For current pricing information,
or to learn more about this or any Nextext title,
call us toll-free at **1-800-323-5435**
or visit our web site at www.nextext.com.

D1072197

A HISTORICAL READER

The Irish Americans

nextext

Edited by: James V. Mullin

President, Irish Famine Curriculum Committee; Member,
New Jersey Commission on Holocaust Education.

Cover photograph: Irish immigrants arriving in America via 20th-century
steamship. Courtesy of Culver Pictures.

Printed in the United States of America

ISBN 0-618-04819-7

1 2 3 4 5 6 7 — QKT — 06 05 04 03 02 01 00

Table of Contents

PART III: OPPORTUNITIES AND RESPONSIBILITIES

PART IV: PROSE, POETRY, SONGS, AND STEREOTYPES

Throughout the reader, vocabulary words appear in boldface type and are footnoted. Specialized or technical words and phrases appear in lightface type and are footnoted.

Ireland

Four Provinces, Thirty-two Counties Ireland is the most westerly of the countries of Europe. It covers an area of 32,524 square miles, about the size of the state of Maine. Historically, Ireland has been divided into four provinces: Leinster, Munster, Connacht, and Ulster. The first three of these provinces, along with the traditional Ulster counties of Donegal, Monaghan and Cavan, make up the twenty-six county Republic of Ireland, with its capital at Dublin. When Ireland was partitioned in 1922, the remaining six counties of Ulster became Northern Ireland, a part of the United Kingdom, with its capital at Belfast.

Coming to America

Saving Civilization

BY THOMAS CAHILL

Ireland is sometimes referred to as "the land of saints and scholars" because of the work of Irish monks during the "Dark Ages." After the fall of Rome about 410 A.D., culture, learning, and scholarship disappeared from the European continent for centuries, and great libraries were destroyed by illiterate barbarians. The Greek, Roman, Jewish, and Christian classics might have been lost forever, if not for Irish monks and scribes who laboriously and lovingly preserved them. The spiritual lives of these men and women inspired their art and work, and they taught Latin and Greek to Irish and non-Irish alike. Their exacting calligraphy was a form of prayer, and their beautiful books and illuminated manuscripts represent Ireland's golden age of art and scholarship, as classics scholar Cahill explains in this excerpt from his best-selling book, How the Irish Saved Civilization.

The word *Irish* is seldom coupled with the word *civilization*. When we think of peoples as civilized or civilizing, the Egyptians and the Greeks, the Italians and the French, the Chinese and the Jews may all come to mind. The Irish are wild, **feckless**,[1] and charming, or **morose**,[2] repressed, and corrupt, but not especially civilized. If we strain to think of "Irish civilization," no image appears, no Fertile Crescent or Indus Valley,[3] no brooding bust of Beethoven. . . .

And yet . . . Ireland, a little island at the edge of Europe that has known neither Renaissance nor Enlightenment—in some ways, a Third World country with, as John Betjeman[4] claimed, a Stone Age culture—had one moment of unblemished glory. For, as the Roman Empire fell, as all through Europe matted, unwashed barbarians descended on the Roman cities, looting artifacts and burning books, the Irish, who were just learning to read and write, took up the great labor of copying all of Western literature—everything they could lay their hands on. These scribes then served as **conduits**[5] through which the Greco-Roman and Judeo-Christian cultures were transmitted to the tribes of Europe, newly settled amid the rubble and ruined vineyards of the civilization they had overwhelmed. Without this Service of the Scribes, everything that happened subsequently would have been unthinkable. Without the Mission of the Irish Monks, who single-handedly refounded European civilization throughout the continent in the bays and valleys of their exile, the world that came after them would have been an entirely different one—a world without books. And our own world would never have come to be.

Not for a thousand years—not since the Spartan Legion had perished at the Hot Gates of Thermopylae[6]—

---

[1] **feckless**—careless, irresponsible, or lacking in purpose.

[2] **morose**—gloomy or ill-humored.

[3] Fertile Crescent or Indus Valley—areas of the world, the first in modern-day Iraq and the second in India, where two of the earliest civilizations surfaced.

[4] John Betjeman—poet who wrote about Ireland.

[5] **conduits**—channels.

[6] Hot Gates of Thermopylae—battle in ancient Greece in 480 B.C. in which Spartans heroically defended a narrow pass against invading Persians.

had western civilization been put to such a test or faced such odds, nor would it again face extinction till in this century it devised the means of extinguishing all life. As our story opens at the beginning of the fifth century, no one could foresee the coming collapse. But to reasonable men in the second half of the century, surveying the situation of their time, the end was no longer in doubt: their world was finished. One could do nothing but, like Ausonius,[7] retire to one's villa, write poetry, and await the inevitable. It never occurred to them that the building blocks of their world would be saved by outlandish oddities from a land so **marginal**[8] that the Romans had not bothered to conquer it, by men so strange they lived in little huts on rocky outcrops and shaved half their heads and tortured themselves with fasts and chills and nettle baths.[9] As [cultural historian] Kenneth Clark said, "Looking back from the great civilizations of twelfth-century France or seventeenth-century Rome, it is hard to believe that for quite a long time—almost a hundred years—western Christianity survived by clinging to places like Skellig Michael, a pinnacle of rock eighteen miles from the Irish coast, rising seven hundred feet out of the sea."

Clark, who began his *Civilisation* with a chapter (called "The Skin of Our Teeth") on the **precarious**[10] transition from classical to medieval, is an exception in that he gives full weight to the Irish contribution. Many historians fail to mention it entirely, and few **advert**[11] to the breathtaking drama of this cultural cliffhanger. This is probably because it is easier to describe **stasis**[12] (classical, *then* medieval)

---

[7] Ausonius—fourth-century A.D. Roman poet and teacher who lived on his estate in what is now France.

[8] **marginal**—barely acceptable for farming.

[9] nettle baths—baths in which the monks scrub themselves with the leaves of the nettle plant, which gives off a substance that irritates the skin.

[10] **precarious**—difficult; dangerous.

[11] **advert**—call attention.

[12] **stasis**—a standstill, or condition of motionlessness.

than movement (classical *to* medieval). It is also true that historians are generally expert in one period or the other, so that analysis of the transition falls outside their—and everyone's?—competence. At all events, I know of no single book now in print that is devoted to the subject of the transition, nor even one in which this subject plays a substantial part.

In looking to remedy this omission, we may as well ask ourselves the big question: How real is history? Is it just an enormous soup, so full of **disparate**[13] ingredients that it is uncharacterizable? Is it true, as [historian] Emil Cioran has remarked, that history proves nothing because it contains everything? Is not the reverse side of this that history can be made to say whatever we wish it to?

I think, rather, that every age writes history anew, reviewing deeds and texts of other ages from its own vantage point. Our history, the history we read in school and refer to in later life, was largely written by Protestant Englishmen and Anglo-Saxon Protestant Americans. Just as certain contemporary historians have been discovering that such **redactors**[14] are not always reliable when it comes to the contributions of, say, women or African Americans, we should not be surprised to find that such storytellers have overlooked a tremendous contribution in the distant past that was both Celtic and Catholic, a contribution without which European civilization would have been impossible.

---

[13] **disparate**—different.
[14] **redactors**—editors.

QUESTIONS TO CONSIDER

1. How was civilization passed on before the invention of the printing press?

2. How might a break of several hundred years affect the passing on of culture from generation to generation?

3. What made the transition from classical to medieval so difficult and uncertain?

4. Why does Cahill consider it vitally important for us to consider who wrote the historical narratives we are reading, especially when we are weighing the contributions of various peoples?

The Irish in Early America

BY ANN KATHLEEN BRADLEY

The Irish were among the earliest settlers in England's American colonies. They experienced the great difficulties of crossing the Atlantic and adjusting to a new way of life that most early settlers experienced. They made their place in history as farmers and tradesmen, printers and lawyers, soldiers against the British in the American Revolution, signers of the Declaration of Independence. A son of Irish immigrants served as President of the nation in its early years. Later, as more came, the established residents created organizations to help them, even as anti-immigrant prejudice was born. Historian Ann Kathleen Bradley tells their story in the following excerpt from her book History of the Irish in America.

Driven by increasing economic and political pressures at home, and lured by the prospect of independence and even prosperity in the New World, as many as 100,000 Irish traveled to the North American colonies before 1700, and up to four times that number decided to try their luck across the ocean in the century that followed. Perhaps three-fourths of the immigrants before 1700 were Catholics, but during the next century many more Protestant Dissenters[1]—especially Ulster[2] Presbyterians—and even Anglicans swelled the exodus to North America.

A large number of the poorer emigrants came as indentured servants. In exchange for free passage and promises of some sort of **recompense**[3] when they had fulfilled their obligation, they agreed to spend a specified number of years working for the master who paid their way across, fed and clothed them after they arrived, and sometimes taught them a trade. In the labor-hungry colonies this arrangement was particularly **advantageous**[4] for the prospective master, who could often get an indentured servant for an eighth the wages he would have had to pay a "native born." In 1678, a hundred Irish families who had indentured themselves in order to begin again in the New World arrived in Virginia and the Carolinas from Barbados.

Other emigrants came as "redemptioners," who were entitled to repay their passage when they landed if they could collect the money, sometimes from friends or family already living in the colonies. Wealthier merchants or farmers might recruit servants to go with them on the voyage. And a small number of emigrants paid their own fare—an amount equal to over a year's wages for the poor laborers and farmhands.

The trip across was not an easy one. Particularly during the seventeenth century, up to a third of the voyagers often perished, either during the passage or during the first year's "seasoning." In 1670 Virginia's

---

[1] Dissenters—those who refused to conform to the doctrines of the established church, the Protestant Church of Ireland (which was an offshoot of the Church of England or Anglican Church).

[2] Ulster—the most northern of Ireland's four provinces and the only one where Protestants (most of them descendants of Scottish or English families) outnumbered Roman Catholics.

[3] **recompense**—pay or reward for service.

[4] **advantageous**—beneficial.

governor reported that a full four-fifths of the indentured servants died soon after they arrived from disease, harsh weather or overwork. Conditions in the ship's hold, where poor passengers were confined, were cramped, overcrowded, and unsanitary. Food and water onboard were generally inadequate, and many passengers, already weak and undernourished, **succumbed**[5] to typhus, scurvy and other diseases.

Even if they survived the voyage over, these earliest immigrants often found their new land a difficult place to put down roots. They had come from a tightly knit society, where families worked their few acres together. Villagers in the *clachans,* the rural farming communities, traditionally shared implements and supplies and helped each other with building, sowing and harvesting. Families were close-knit and loyal, and family members felt a strong responsibility to share whatever they had with each other.

Colonial masters, however, did not always feel obligated to fulfill their part of even the written indenture agreement. Whereas in Ireland a wide array of unspoken obligations had been supported and maintained by tradition and public opinion, the colonial laws protecting servants were usually inadequate and were a poor defense against greedy masters with property and education on their side. One servant girl in Maryland wrote home that

I . . . am toiling almost day and night, . . . then tied up and whipped to that degree that you'd not serve an animal. [We have] scarce anything but Indian corn and salt to eat, and that even begrudged. Nay, many negroes are better used. [We are] almost naked, no shoes nor stockings to wear. And . . . after slaving during Master's pleasure, what rest we can get is to wrap ourselves in a blanket and lie upon the ground.

---

[5] **succumbed**—fell victim to.

She then begged her father, "if you have any bowels of compassion left," to send her some clothing. Colonial newspapers of the day carried many advertisements for Irish servants or apprentices who ran away to try to escape such conditions.

For those who managed to endure, however, and finish out their period of indenture, there was always the chance of financial and social acceptance and success. As one emigrant wrote in a letter home in 1737: "There is servants comes here out of Ereland, who are now Justices of the Piece. . . ."

Most of those who came to the colonies as indentured servants were single men, but there were a number of single women as well. Few poor families could afford to make the trip together, although some families did travel from Ulster, often as part of whole congregations fleeing Anglican[6] persecution. The single laborers were usually children of impoverished farmers or farmhands, although some were prisoners convicted of crimes— often acts of rebellion against the British—or even the victims of greedy merchants and shipmasters, who kidnapped and then transported their human cargo to America before auctioning them off as servants to the highest bidders. The young colonies' almost **insatiable**[7] need for laborers unfortunately encouraged such unscrupulous practices.

Although most emigrants came from rural farming communities, lack of funds and the forbidding loneliness of the American frontier kept many from trying to begin again on the land. This letter home, written by an Irish farmer who had shaped a homestead from the Missouri wilderness, contrasts the life there with the one he had left:

---

[6] Anglican—referring to the Church of England and its offshoot, the Church of Ireland.

[7] **insatiable**—never-satisfied; unending.

I could then [in Ireland] go to a fair, or a wake, or a dance. . . . I could spend the winter's nights in a neighbor's house cracking jokes by the turf fire. If I had there but a sore head I could have a neighbor within every hundred yards of me that would run to see me. But here everyone can get so much land . . . that they calls them neighbors that live two or three miles off.

For those who, like this man, decided to give farming a try, land was a bargain: an acre of fertile frontier terrain could be bought for the same amount it cost to rent an often overworked acre of farmland in Ireland. Virginia and Maryland were popular destinations, and areas named "New Munster"[8] and "New Ireland" testified to the origin of their settlers. Anglo-Irish[9] families such as the Butlers and the Lynches founded prosperous plantations along Chesapeake Bay and the coasts of the Carolinas. One well-known "Irish Tract" ran through the Shenandoah Valley. Ulster Irish occupied Ulster County in New York's Mohawk Valley and carved out farms from the rich soil of Pennsylvania and New Jersey, gradually moving west and south into the frontier wilderness of Virginia, the Carolinas and Georgia. They wore fringed hunting shirts and moccasins, and built themselves log cabins with earthen floors. But they also founded schools to train ministers for their Presbyterian churches—among them such universities as Princeton, Dickinson, Washington and Jefferson, Allegheny and Hampden-Sydney. The plantation economies of the West Indies also needed agricultural workers, but many of the Irish who settled—or were sent there by Cromwell[10]— eventually made their way to the mainland. Merchants and tradesmen and their servants, on the other hand,

---

[8] Munster—the most southern of Ireland's four provinces.

[9] Anglo-Irish—descendants of English settlers in Ireland, who usually were prosperous Protestant landowners.

[10] Cromwell—Oliver Cromwell (1599–1658), the leader of Puritan-dominated England in the mid-1600s, who personally led an invasion of Ireland in part to suppress Catholicism.

swelled the populations of the large and growing towns along the eastern seaboard, such as New York, Philadelphia and Boston, where a bustling trade had grown up that exchanged Irish provisions and textiles for Chesapeake tobacco and West Indian sugar . . . .

On March 5, 1770, British troops fired on protesting natives in the streets of Boston, an event that American rebels were soon calling the "Boston Massacre." Among the five men killed that day was Patrick Carr, an Irishman. This event symbolized the sympathy many Irish, those still in the homeland as well as those who had emigrated, felt for the young Colonies' gathering revolt against their common enemy, the British.

Many who had already settled in the Colonies joined the Continental army and fought valiantly for the American cause, although others, particularly those who had been granted land and positions by the King, remained loyal to and fought for the [British] Crown. . . .

The majority of Americans of Irish heritage, however, felt strong sympathy for the radicals in their fight for independence, and a number distinguished themselves as officers under General Washington. As many as one-third to one-half the colonial troops were probably either born in Ireland or had Irish parents, including 1,492 officers and 26 generals, of whom 15 were Irish-born. [British] General Sir Henry Clinton summed up the fervor of the Irish patriots when he declared that "the emigrants from Ireland are in general . . . our most serious **antagonists**."[11]

Among the many noted Irish officers was John Sullivan, whose father had emigrated from Limerick in 1723. Sullivan was hailed as "the first to take up arms against the King" after he led New Hampshire militia-men in an attack on Fort William and Mary in Newcastle, New Hampshire, in 1774. The gunpowder

---

[11] **antagonists**—opponents or adversaries.

they captured there was later used at the Battle of Bunker Hill. Sullivan was a major-general in the Continental Army and later, in 1779, he defeated the alliance of the Iroquois and [pro-British] Loyalists in New York State. General Richard Montgomery, a native of Dublin, invaded Canada and captured Montreal before being killed in an attack on Quebec City in December 1775. Another officer of Irish birth, Andrew Lewis, had actually served as a colonel in the British army before joining the patriots in 1776 as a brigadier general.[12] While in the service of the British he had defeated the Shawnee Indians at Point Pleasant, a strategically important spot on the Ohio River, thus opening up the Northwest Territory to American penetration after the outbreak of the Revolution. Irish sharpshooter Timothy Murphy of Morgan's Rifle Corps was the son of immigrants and was to become the most famous marksman of the Revolution. He put the colonists a large step closer to victory when he killed two British commanders during the Battle of Saratoga. Even George Washington's most important "confidential agent" was an Irish-born tailor named Hercules Mulligan. By serving as a double agent while the British occupied New York, Mulligan was able to gather much valuable information on enemy strategy for the Patriot cause.

It was not just on land that Irish warriors distinguished themselves during the American fight for independence. Many fought valiantly for the cause at sea. Jeremiah O'Brien, whose father came from Cork, captured the British schooner *Margaretta* off the coast of Maine on June 12, 1775, in the first naval battle of the Revolution. Another Irish-American revolutionary hero, Wexford-born John Barry, became the "Father of the United States Navy" when he was commissioned its commodore in February 1797, after outstanding service during the War of Independence.

---

[12] brigadier general—commissioned officer above the rank of colonel and below a major general.

The valor of the many Irish enlisted men in the Continental army was also crucial to the success of the American cause. Among them was Andrew Jackson, the son of immigrants from County Antrim, who was later elected President of the young republic. After seeing duty as a soldier during the Revolution, Jackson went on to fight the British a second time during the War of 1812, when he won a major victory as commander at the Battle of New Orleans. He is honored by the American Irish as a great soldier, leader, and friend of the common man.

On the day the British evacuated Boston—March 17, 1776—General Washington acknowledged the invaluable support of his many Irish officers and men by designating "St. Patrick" the password of the day. Soon after, on July 4, 1776, the break with England became **irrevocable**[13] when members of the Continental Congress signed the Declaration of Independence. Three native-born Irish were among the signers—Dubliner James Smith, a lawyer, redemptioner George Taylor, both of Pennsylvania; and Matthew Thornton of New Hampshire, a physician, who had emigrated with his parents when he was three. Signers of Irish descent included Charles Carroll, the only Catholic (whose family had dropped the initial "O" from their name), Thomas Lynch, Thomas McKean, George Read and Edward Rutledge. The Secretary of the Continental Congress, Charles Thomson, whose duty it was to read the Declaration to that body for the first time, was also Irish-born. After his parents died, Thomson left Derry as an indentured servant at the age of 10, and rose in less than 20 years to become a well-to-do merchant in the thriving commercial city of Philadelphia.

In addition, the printer to Congress who printed the document, John Dunlap, had come to America from County Tyrone in 1757; in 1771 he founded

---

[13] **irrevocable**—irreversible.

The Pennsylvania Packet. A weekly when it first began publication, *The Packet* later became the first daily newspaper to be published in the new United States.

Many Irish, both at home and in the Colonies, applauded the American revolt as a struggle against their common enemy, the British. . . .

At the same time, the end of hostilities between Britain and America unleashed a flood of new emigrants from Irish shores—perhaps as many as 150,000 left between 1783 and 1814. The trade in Irish servants declined because captains of British ships could no longer be certain American courts would uphold contracts of indenture. . . .

As a result, most of those who left Ireland for America during this period were successful farmers, skilled craftsmen, or businessmen, and professionals—merchants, clerks, schoolmasters, doctors, and their families.

To help these growing numbers of immigrants adjust to life in their new country, some of the more affluent and established Irish-American residents created organizations such as the Charitable Irish Society in Boston and the Society for the Relief of Emigrants from Ireland, which was begun in Philadelphia in 1793—the favorite port of entry and the same city whose flourishing Irish community had started a Hibernian Society[14] in 1790. Among the founders of the former was Matthew Carey, a prominent publisher, bookseller, and intellectual leader, who had been a noted newspaper editor in Dublin before escaping to America to avoid prosecution for speaking out against the Crown. A Benevolent Hibernian Society was founded in Baltimore in 1803, and in 1814 New York's Irish community created its own Irish Emigrant Society to protect and assist new arrivals.

Even as Irish-Americans in the United States were organizing to welcome and assist their newly arrived fellow countrymen, however, the government of the

---

[14] Hibernian Society—social club for Irish immigrants and their descendants. *Hibernia* is a Latin name given to Ireland by the ancient Romans.

new nation was taking steps to restrict and regulate the **influx**[15] of immigrants. After the French Revolution and the 1798 United Irish uprising,[16] many political refugees sought asylum in America. Fearing the spread of extremist ideas, which might **abet**[17] the domestic republicanism of radical representatives such as County Wicklow-born Matthew Lyon of Vermont, the American Federalist Party passed laws that extended the required residence period for citizenship from five to fourteen years and gave the President the right to expel "dangerous" aliens by executive decree. "If some means are not adopted," insisted Massachusetts Congressman Harrison Gray Otis in 1797, "to prevent the indiscriminate admission of wild Irishmen and others to the right of suffrage, there will . . . be an end to liberty and property." A third such law, called the Sedition Act, declared it a misdemeanor to make statements "with the intent to defame" Congress and the President, or statements that might bring them into "contempt or disrepute." Lyon, an ardent admirer of Jefferson and the French Revolution, was the first to be prosecuted.

Among those who emigrated at this time was James McKinley of County Antrim, grandfather of President William McKinley, who left after his brother Francis was hanged as a United Irish rebel. Many rebel leaders fled as well to escape prosecution and execution for treason, including Thomas Addis Emmet, older brother of condemned revolutionary Robert Emmet, who was hanged by the British for his defiant nationalism after he led an unsuccessful rebellion in 1803. The courageous speech he delivered at his trial made him a popular hero on both sides of the Atlantic. The elder Emmet, who had

---

[15] **influx**—inflow.

[16] the 1798 United Irish uprising—an unsuccessful revolt against British rule in Ireland involving both Catholic and Protestant Irishmen and their French allies.

[17] **abet**—assist.

helped found the Society of United Irishmen, was admitted to the New York Bar by a special legislative act. It was the first step in a brilliant political career in New York State, where he eventually served as attorney general. Theobald Wolfe Tone, originator of the concept of violent separatist revolution still advocated by many Irish nationalists, also spent a period of exile in America before returning [in 1798] to arrange for the landing of a French invasion force that was to aid the Irish separatists. He was captured and committed suicide while in prison after his request for an honorable execution before a firing squad was denied.

QUESTIONS TO CONSIDER

1. How were living and working conditions in the New World different from those in Ireland?

2. In what ways did the historical conflict between the English and the Irish play itself out in America?

3. Why was the American Federalist Party afraid of the new immigrants from Europe after the French Revolution and the 1798 United Irish uprising? What ideas did they bring?

4. What is your opinion of a law, like the Sedition Act, that makes it a crime to speak out against the President or Congress?

Great Famine Forever Altered Ireland

BY KERBY MILLER

The Great Famine, 1845–1850, radically altered Ireland's economic, social, and religious landscapes. In this essay Kerby Miller, professor of history at the University of Missouri, author of the important and highly praised Emigrants and Exiles: Ireland and the Irish Exodus to North America, *and co-author of* Out of Ireland, *discusses the causes and consequences of this great disaster. He explains Ireland's pre-Famine poverty environment, the ravages of Famine hunger and disease, the culpability of British officials in the high death toll and the flight of more than two million refugees, and how bitter memories of starvation, sickness, and exile fueled anti-British Irish nationalism on both sides of the Atlantic.*

A mist rose up out of the sea, and you could hear a voice talking near a mile off across the stillness of the earth. It was the same for three days or more, and then, when the fog lifted, you could begin to see the tops of the potato stalks lying over as if the life was gone out of them. And that was the beginning of the great trouble and Famine that destroyed Ireland.

So the Great Famine of 1845–1850 appeared in the memories of elderly men and women who survived Ireland's greatest catastrophe: as a sudden and, at first, an **inexplicable**[1] disaster. Between 1845 and the mid-1850s, when the Famine's immediate effects finally subsided, more than 1 million Irish perished of starvation and disease, some 500,000 were evicted from their homes, and more than 2 million emigrated, primarily to the United States. Between 1841 and 1861, Ireland's population declined from 8.2 million to 5.8 million.

If possible, the long-term effects of the Famine were even more profound. Ireland's population never recovered. Between 1861 and 1926 over 4 million more Irishmen and women went overseas, and by 1926, the island had only 4.2 million inhabitants. The "Great Hunger" of 1845–50 dramatically altered Irish Catholic society and culture. The ranks of the Irish peasantry— the small farmers and laborers who had transmitted the island's rich Gaelic culture, its stories, songs and poems from generation to generation—were **decimated**[2] by deaths and departures.

Prior to the Famine, at least half of Ireland's Catholics still spoke Irish (or Gaelic) as their primary or only language. But by 1851, only 23 percent and by 1901 merely 14 percent of Ireland's people could speak their native tongue. A treasure of lore and legend was lost forever.

In recent decades, it has been fashionable for Irish historians to downplay or ignore the political reasons for Irish distress. Nevertheless, Ireland's colonial status in the British Empire and British prejudices against Irish Catholics surely contributed to Irish misery, both before and during the Great Famine.

---

[1] **inexplicable**—not possible to explain.
[2] **decimated**—nearly destroyed.

In 1690, the victory of King William III at the Battle of the Boyne had sealed the English/Protestant conquest of Ireland. By the early 1700s about 90 percent of Irish land had been granted to Protestant landlords, reducing nearly all Catholics to the status of tenants and laborers. In the same period, a series of Penal Laws were passed to make Catholics impoverished and submissive. By the 1790s, most Penal Laws had been relaxed or repealed, but Catholics were still forbidden to hold political offices until 1829, and the Laws' economic and psychological effects lingered for generations. Not until the early 20th century did British legislation finally enable most Irish tenants to purchase from their landlords the farms their ancestors had lost. But the abolition of Irish landlordism came too late to benefit the victims of the Great Famine.

Between 1750 and 1821, Ireland experienced an explosive increase in population, from about 2.3 million to 6.8 million. Thereafter, the rate of growth slowed, thanks largely to increased emigration. During the three decades prior to the Famine nearly one million Irish went overseas, more than double the number of emigrants in the preceding two centuries, yet in 1845 Ireland still had about 8.5 million inhabitants. However, Ireland's **burgeoning**[3] population alone was not the Famine's root cause. After all, during the same period Britain's population increased at an even faster rate, to a much higher level. The primary problems were economic ones which stemmed from the profound inequities of Irish rural society, which, in turn, reflected the **pervasive**[4] consequences of British conquest, confiscation, and colonization.

In the early 19th century, a few hundred families, nearly all Protestants, owned most of the land. Many Protestant landlords were absentees, living in Britain, who regarded their Irish estates merely as sources of income

---

[3] **burgeoning**—rapidly growing.

[4] **pervasive**—thoroughly widespread.

and who rented their lands to **parasitical**[5] "middlemen" who, in turn, sublet the soil to the actual cultivators.

Desperate poverty, even before Famine

During the decades before the Famine, the small farmers and the laborers, who together comprised nearly three-fourths of Ireland's rural population, usually lived in desperate poverty: dressed in rags, without shoes, inhabiting thatched mud-walled, earth-floored cabins with little furniture or bedding; subsisting largely or entirely on the produce of their potato gardens; and, when their potato crops failed, subject to starvation and to the diseases that accompanied malnutrition. After 1815, their **plight**[6] was worsened not only by their increasing numbers but also by a severe economic depression that sharply reduced the prices of farm produce and devastated cottage industries. At the same time, rents remained high.

The Irish countryside today is characterized by isolated, compact farms. But in the late 18th and the early 19th centuries, most poor Catholics still lived in crowded rural settlements called *clachans*. A few dozen, or even several hundred, one or two-room thatched cabins were clustered together, surrounded by a multitude of tiny, unfenced fields, for raising potatoes or oats and for grazing **stunted**[7] livestock. The peasants who lived in the *clachans* were wretchedly poor, and their villages usually lacked shops, markets, churches, public buildings, and other amenities. However, the *clachans* were the vital centers of rural Irish social and cultural life.

When potato crops were abundant, and when they could earn a little cash to pay rents from selling butter or

---

[5] **parasitical**—like parasites; those who live off others for their own gain while providing nothing in return.

[6] **plight**—unfortunate condition.

[7] **stunted**—unnaturally small and slowed in growth.

pigs, the villagers were virtually self-sufficient. For each *clachan* contained families whose weaving, shoemaking, thatching, and other skills provided most of life's necessities. And each also contained the traditional musicians, singers, poets and storytellers who gave life meaning, continuity and joy.

In retrospect, one can argue that the Irish peasants' impoverished yet **vibrant**[8] world was inevitably doomed to destruction. Indeed, in the early 19th century, the *clachans* and the traditional culture that they sustained were already vanishing. But the peasants resisted, forming secret **agrarian**[9] societies, such as the Whiteboys and the Molly Maguires, which countered evictions, high rents and other oppressions with nocturnal campaigns of **intimidation**[10] and violence. Had it not been for the Famine, Ireland's depopulation and the Anglicization[11] of Irish rural culture would have proceeded only at a slow, steady but perhaps reversible pace.

But in August 1845, the Irish potato crop was blighted by the hitherto-unknown fungus *Phytophthora infestans*, and for five successive years the peasants' major food source failed totally or partly. The result was mass starvation on a scale not witnessed in the British Isles or in Western Europe for more than 100 years.

Hundreds of thousands of peasants starved to death in their cabins or by the roadsides, their mouths stained green by the grass they had eaten in a vain attempt to stay alive. Others crawled into Irish towns, seeking shelter in the poor houses the British government had begun constructing in 1838. They were soon crowded to overflowing with the dead and dying. Still others wandered about, frantically searching for food or work, spreading typhus, cholera and other diseases. The worst year was

---

[8] **vibrant**—pulsating with energy.

[9] **agrarian**—rural; agricultural.

[10] **intimidation**—actions causing fear.

[11] Anglicization—making something English in form, style, or character.

1847—Black '47—when hundreds of thousands perished. But 1848 and 1849 were nearly as bad. The "hidden Ireland" of the *clachans* was swept away.

The inadequacy of British relief

Government relief was constrained by British officials' devotion to *laissez faire* doctrines[12]—which prescribed that the provision of food and work should be left to private entrepreneurs and to the natural laws of supply and demand—as well as by **inveterate**[13] anti-Irish prejudices. The *London Times* declared the Famine "a great blessing," a "valuable opportunity for settling" once and for all "the **vexed**[14] question of Irish-discontent."

As a result of such opinions, British relief was grossly inadequate. Shiploads of American corn were sent to Ireland while large amounts of Irish foodstuffs were shipped out of the island to the British market. The peasants lacked cash to purchase the imported cornmeal, yet the wages which the government paid them for laboring on road-building and other relief projects were often too little, or paid too late, to **avert**[15] starvation.

For millions, emigration overseas represented their best, perhaps their only, chance of escaping **destitution**[16] and death. The poorest Irish lacked the means to pay for passage to North America, and the British government refused pleas for financial assistance to emigrate, even to British colonies.

Despite their poverty, hundreds of thousands in North America helped bring their kinsmen and women to Quebec, New York, Boston, Philadelphia, New Orleans and other destinations.

---

[12] *laissez-faire* doctrines—principles of government that hold that commerce should not be interfered with.

[13] **inveterate**—deeply-rooted or ingrained.

[14] **vexed**—irritating or annoying.

[15] **avert**—prevent; avoid.

[16] **destitution**—extreme poverty.

For those Irish lucky enough to escape Ireland, however, the horrors of the Famine were often compounded by the terrors of the crossing. Ships commonly sailed without adequate water provisions, medical assistance, or cooking and sanitary facilities.

Voyages usually lasted five to six weeks, but passages of more than twice that length were not unusual. Many Famine emigrants were not only weakened by malnutrition when they embarked but also carried the germs of typhus and dysentery into their cramped and **fetid**[17] steerage quarters. During Black '47, mortality rates aboard the "coffin ships" were as high as 40 percent. Including those who died in the slums of North American cities, or in quarantine camps such as the one on Grosse Isle near Quebec, as many as 50,000 Irish died en route to the U.S. and Canada.

Lasting scar on Irish at home and abroad

The Famine left a deep and lasting scar not only on the Irish in Ireland but on the Irish in North America, searing its survivors with vivid and bitter memories. Although priests generally attributed the Famine to an "act of God," a divine affliction sent to punish the people for their sins, the Irish in the U.S. laid the blame on the British government and on Ireland's Protestant landlords. Many vowed revenge, and in the late nineteenth and early twentieth centuries their hatred for England and for Irish landlordism inspired the Irish overseas to send millions of dollars to support Irish nationalist movements.

The Land War of 1879–82, the Easter Rising of 1916, the partly successful War for Irish Independence of 1919–21, which created what is now the Irish Republic—all these were financed by Irish-American donations, which in turn were generated by the Famine's bitter legacy.

---

[17] **fetid**—having an offensive smell; stinking.

Indeed, from the late 1960s until the recent, apparent end of violence in Northern Ireland, some American Irish sent money to the Irish Republican Army.[18] Many Irish people in Ireland and, especially, in America have agreed with the fiery nationalist, John Mitchel, who declared, "The Almighty, indeed, sent the potato blight, but the English created the Famine."

Ireland's tragedy—a summary

In August 1845, the Irish potato crop was blighted by a previously unknown fungus. For five years, the peasants' major food source was ruined.

The Famine, through starvation and disease, killed more than 1 million Irishmen and women.

Unable to pay rent, more than a half-million men, women and children were evicted from their cottages.

Between the mid-1800's and 1926, more than 6 million Irishmen and Irishwomen went overseas.

By 1926, the island had 4.2 million inhabitants, down from 8.2 million before the Famine began.

---

[18] Irish Republican Army—underground military organization that uses terrorist tactics to try to unite Northern Ireland, which is part of the British United Kingdom, with the independent Republic of Ireland.

QUESTIONS TO CONSIDER

1. What was the British contribution to the Famine disaster in Ireland?

2. How did the Famine alter Irish life and institutions?

3. How did the Famine fuel anti-British Irish nationalism?

The Famine Year

BY LADY JANE FRANCESCA WILDE

Throughout the mass starvation in Ireland, Britain was guided by laissez faire, or "free market" economic principles. Merchants, speculators, and landlords successfully lobbied the British government to continue to export food from Ireland to England and other places where it would bring the highest prices. In 1845, more than twenty-five million bushels of grain were shipped out of Ireland, and between 1846 and 1850 more than three million live animals were exported. During "Black '47," when four hundred thousand Irish people died of starvation, almost four thousand vessels carrying food left Ireland for ports in Bristol, Glasgow, Liverpool, and London, according to Dr. Christine Kinealy of the University of Liverpool. In nine months of that same year, she says, 1,336,220 gallons of grain-derived alcohol were exported from Ireland, along with 822,681 gallons of butter. The following poem, "The Famine Year," was written in the mid-nineteenth century by an angry Anglo-Irish poet, Jane Francesca Wilde, the mother of wit and playwright Oscar Wilde.

Weary men, what reap ye?—Golden corn for the stranger.

What sow ye?—Human corses[1] that wait for the avenger.

Fainting forms, hunger-stricken, what see you in the offing?[2]

Stately ships to bear our food away, amid the stranger's scoffing.

There's a proud array[3] of soldiers—what do they round your door?

They guard our masters' granaries[4] from the thin hands of the poor.

Pale mothers, wherefore weeping—Would to God that we were dead;

Our children swoon before us, and we cannot give them bread.

---

[1] corses—corpses.

[2] offing—the near or immediate future.

[3] array—orderly arrangement.

[4] granaries—places to store grain.

QUESTIONS TO CONSIDER

1. Why do the people in Lady Wilde's poem believe the food being exported is theirs?

2. How would an absentee landlord's point of view differ from theirs?

3. How effective, in your opinion, is the question-and-answer format of the poem?

Wretched Conditions on Emigrant Ships

BY ROBERT SMITH

*In 1847, the British government passed laws taxing landlords
in Ireland to pay for the relief of their starving tenants. Landlords
understood that the cost of keeping a tenant in the workhouse
for one year was generally about twice the cost of the fare to the
Americas. Therefore, it was to the landlords' economic advantage
to book passage for their poorest tenants. The cheapest passage
was on board "coffin ships" headed for British colonies in Canada.
Robert Smith traveled for two months on board an emigrant ship
bound for Canada, and he stayed in steerage, the cheapest passenger accommodation, in order to experience the voyage of the
poorest emigrant firsthand. Smith returned to London in 1847 and
gave the following testimony before a Select Committee of the
House of Lords, the upper chamber of the British Parliament. He told
the committee members that the regulations for ensuring passenger
health were not, and could not be, enforced.*

Minutes of evidence before the Select Committee (Lords) on Emigration from Ireland.

The fearful state of disease and debility in which the Irish emigrants have reached Canada must undoubtedly be attributed in a great degree to the **destitution**[1] and consequent sickness prevailing in Ireland, but has been much aggravated by the neglect of cleanliness, ventilation and a generally good state of social economy during the passage, and has afterwards been increased and **disseminated**[2] throughout the whole country in the mal-arrangements of the Government system of emigrant relief. . . .

Before the emigrant has been a week at sea he is an altered man. How can it be otherwise? Hundreds of poor people, men, women and children of all ages, from the drivelling idiot of ninety to the babe just born, huddled together without light, without air, wallowing in filth and breathing a **fetid**[3] atmosphere, sick in body, dispirited in heart, the fever patients lying between the sound, in sleeping places so narrow as almost to deny them the power of indulging, by a change of position, that natural restlessness of the disease; by their ravings disturbing those around, and predisposing them, through the effects of the imagination, to **imbibe**[4] the contagion; living without food or medicine, except as administered by the hand of casual charity, dying without the voice of spiritual consolation, and buried in deep[5] without the rites of the Church. The food is generally ill-selected and seldom sufficiently cooked; in consequence of the supply of water, hardly enough for cooking and drinking, does not allow washing. In many ships the filthy beds, teeming with all **abominations**,[6] are never required to be brought

---

[1] **destitution**—extreme poverty.

[2] **disseminated**—spread.

[3] **fetid**—offensive and foul-smelling.

[4] **imbibe**—drink.

[5] buried in deep—buried at sea.

[6] **abominations**—horrors, such as vermin, insects, and filth.

on deck and aired; the narrow space between the sleeping berths and the piles of boxes is never washed or scraped, but breathes up a damp and fetid stench, until the day before the arrival at quarantine, when all hands are required to "scrub up," and put on a fair face for the doctor and Government inspector. No moral restraint is attempted, the voice of prayer is never heard; drunkenness, with its consequent train of **ruffianly debasement**,[7] is not discouraged, because it is profitable to the captain, who traffics in the grog.[8]

In this ship which brought me out from London last April, the passengers were [given] provisions by the owners, according to a contract and a furnished scale of **dietary**.[9]

The meat was of the worst quality. The supply of water shipped on board was abundant, but the quantity served out to the passengers was so scanty that they were frequently obliged to throw overboard their salt provisions and rice (a most important article of their food) because they had not water enough both for the necessary cooking and the satisfying of their raging thirst afterwards.

They could only afford water for washing by withdrawing it from the cooking of their food. I have known persons to remain for days together in their dark, close berths because they thus suffered less from hunger, though compelled at the same time for want of water to heave overboard their salt provisions and rice.

No cleanliness was enforced, and the beds were never aired. The master during the whole voyage never entered the steerage, and would listen to no complaints; the dietary contracted for was, with some exceptions, nominally supplied, though at irregular periods; but false measures were used (in which the water and several

---

[7] **ruffianly debasement**—rough, even violent behavior.

[8] **traffics in the grog**—sells the liquor.

[9] **dietary**—food supplies.

articles of dry food were served), the gallon measure containing but three quarts, which fact I proved in Quebec and had the captain fined for. Once or twice a week **ardent spirits**[10] were sold indiscriminately to the passengers, producing scenes of unchecked **blackguardism**[11] beyond description; and lights were prohibited because the ship—with her open fire-grates upon deck—[and] with lucifer matches[12] and lighted pipes used secretly in the sleeping berths—was freighted with Government powder[13] for the garrison at Quebec.

The case of this ship was not one of peculiar misconduct; on the contrary, I have the strongest reason to know, from information I have received from very many emigrants well known to me, who came over this year in different vessels, that this ship was better regulated and more comfortable than many that reached Canada.

Disease and death among the emigrants, nay, the **propagation**[14] of infection throughout Canada, are not the worst consequences of this atrocious system of neglect and ill-usage. A result far worse is to be found in the utter demoralization of the passengers, both male and female, by the filth and **debasement**[15] and disease of two or three months so passed. The emigrant, enfeebled in body and degraded in mind, even though he should have the physical power, has not the heart, has not the will to exert himself. He has lost his self-respect, his elasticity of spirit; he no longer stands erect; he throws himself listlessly upon the daily dole of Government, and in order to earn it carelessly lies for weeks on the contaminated straw of a fever **lazaretto**.[16]

---

[10] **ardent spirits**—liquor.

[11] **blackguardism**—ruffian behavior.

[12] lucifer matches—a brand of wooden matches.

[13] Government powder—gunpowder.

[14] **propagation**—increase or spread.

[15] **debasement**—lowering in character or dignity.

[16] **lazaretto**—hospital treating contagious diseases.

QUESTIONS TO CONSIDER

1. What conditions in Ireland may have weakened the emigrants even before they boarded the ships?

2. What conditions on board the emigrant ships does Smith say contribute to "altering" the Irish emigrants?

3. Which conditions do you believe are the most likely to contribute to illness, even death?

4. Do you believe Smith's testimony is accurate? Why?

From the Frying Pan into the Fire

BY EDWARD WAKIN

For the Irish country people fleeing the Great Famine, the end of the horrible trans-Atlantic voyage brought them to another crisis: how were they to survive the perils of New York, Boston, or whatever American or Canadian port they had reached? Their welcoming party was a mob of "runners" who fell upon the immigrants even before they left the ship. These were con-men who grabbed luggage and immigrants and tried to drag them to their favorite rooming houses, where they extorted outrageous payments for carrying luggage. The runners frequently sold forged tickets for inland travel, stole trunks from passengers, and generally fleeced the newcomers in any way possible. The runners were also paid for luring new arrivals to rooming houses and saloons, where they would be overcharged, robbed, or short-changed. This was only the beginning of the Irish immigrants' painful experience, as historian Edward Wakin describes.

In general, ships' captains treated their steerage passengers as they did any other cargo—to be unloaded as soon as possible. The only obstacle was the required inspection by a doctor who placed ships in thirty days' quarantine if they were dangerous to the city's health. Since this prospect appealed to neither the captain nor the passengers, steerage passengers had to scrub down their quarters on the eve of arrival, while the captain did his best to hide the lame, the **halt**,[1] and the diseased. Actually, the overworked medical inspectors could not really examine anyone thoroughly. They could only look around and try to spot obvious signs of sickness.

Once past quarantine, the ships unloaded their passengers either by sending them ashore on light boats or by going directly into dock. Then it was up to the arrivals, their luck, their friends, and their personal resources to face the pitfalls. In New York, where the great majority of Irish immigrants landed, they found a city of new splendor and old **squalor**.[2] Pigs roamed the streets and violence was common, while the elegant could dine at Delmonico's or buy a Titian[3] or a Rubens[4] on Broadway. Besides London and Paris, the other great city in the Western world was New York, whose population was being inflated by economic success and immigration—doubling to six hundred and thirty thousand between 1840 and 1855.

As many as thirty or forty ships carrying immigrants might arrive in New York on a single day and the din of their arrival could be heard all over lower Manhattan. The influx was much more than the city could properly handle, particularly a haphazardly-run city like New York. Reluctant, reserved Boston, only one-third the size of New York, was hardest hit by immigration. Whereas only five thousand five hundred immigrants had arrived in the nine years prior to 1845, thirty-seven thousand arrived in the single year 1847. In the mid-1850s, Massachusetts Governor Henry J. Gardner was reflecting

---

[1] **halt**—people unable to walk properly; crippled.

[2] **squalor**—filth, disorder.

[3] Titian—painting by the Italian painter (1477–1576) of the Renaissance period.

[4] Rubens—painting by Peter Paul Rubens (1557–1640), a famous Flemish painter.

the shock and mistrust of native Bostonians when he spoke before his Legislature of the need to "regulate" the newcomers. Whatever the rhetoric or the port of entry, the Irish flowed in with the tide, were tossed up on the shore, and left to their own devices.

Cautiously feeling their way in a strange land, the immigrants had to beware at every step. They were regarded as fair game and were victimized wherever they turned—to exchange money, buy some milk, a coat, a ticket for a canal boat. There were also "hundreds of pickpockets" prowling the piers, as recorded by a mid-century diarist. [Scottish novelist] Robert Louis Stevenson noted in 1879 that he was "at first amused, and then somewhat staggered, by the cautious and grisly tales that went the round" as his ship approached New York's harbor.

Positive action was taken in at least one direction by New York officials, when Castle Garden at the tip of Manhattan was converted into a supervised landing depot—with runners excluded. A thirteen-foot wall was built around what had once been a fort and, beginning August 1, 1855, all immigrants were brought there directly from their ships. Castle Garden was a circular auditorium (billed as the largest in the world) which could hold six thousand to fifteen thousand persons. As a center for entertainment and public meetings, it had housed circuses and **menageries**[5] and was home for [opera singer] Jenny Lind's concerts. For immigrants, it became a haven from sharks, con men, and runners (the latter went to court to claim loss of rights, held protest meetings, and even shot off rockets over Castle Garden—but they lost).

Until 1892 when Ellis Island became the port of entry, immigrants moved through Castle Garden, where their luggage was protected, honest rates of exchange

---

[5] **menageries**—collections of exotic animals.

given for their money, properly-priced rail tickets sold, reputable boarding houses and hotels listed. At times as many as two thousand people slept on the floor of Castle Garden, saving their funds while waiting to move on. There they had wash rooms, free hot water, and milk, bread, cheese, sausages, tea, and coffee at low prices. Officials took in hand children sent alone to join relatives and "with a label fastened around their bodies showing their destination, forwarded them like express parcels."

Already, other labels were being tacked onto the Irishman, sometimes as a figure of fun, at other times of fear. The stage Irishman was played for laughs, done up in tattered rags, thick **brogue**,[6] and heavy-handed absurdities. He boasted, waved a **shillelagh**[7] and, when he spoke, out came *begorra* and *Erin go bragh*.[8] Newspapers set the newcomers apart in stories that referred to "an Irishman" or "a foreigner." As an Irish schoolmaster in New York, Patrick S. Casserly, complained in 1832, "If a swindler, thief, robber, or murderer, no matter what his color or country, commit any **nefarious**[9] or **abominable**[10] act, throughout the Union, he is instantly set down as a native of Ireland."

. . .The Irish were already tarred by the British image of them, as Samuel Griswold Goodrich noted in the 1840s while warning his fellow Americans of the "spell" cast by British books, papers, and pamphlets. They try, he said, to "**vindicate**[11] the tyranny of the government in Ireland, by portraying the Irish as an untamable race, deaf to reason, and only to be ruled by the harsh

---

[6] **brogue**—especially strong Irish accent.

[7] **shillelagh**—walking stick or club, especially one made of oak or blackthorn.

[8] *begorra* and *Erin go bragh*—Gaelic phrases; the first is a mild oath and the second means "Ireland forever."

[9] **nefarious**—infamously evil.

[10] **abominable**—detestable; loathsome.

[11] **vindicate**—clear of accusation, blame, or suspicion.

inflictions of power. Let us, Americans, see that our minds are not driven from the moorings of justice, by this sinister current in which they are placed."

The newly-arrived Irish were making New York their Dublin; indeed a city which would eventually have more Irish inhabitants than Dublin. In 1820, New York City had twenty-five thousand Catholics, most of them Irish; by 1850, it was already one-third Irish (counting the 26 percent who were foreign-born Irish and their offspring in a city of a half-million). Brooklyn, then a separate city, was also gathering in the Irish. Taken together, Brooklyn and New York [City] were more than one-third Irish by the closing decades of the nineteenth century. By 1845, one out of five Bostonians was Irish; a jump from one in fifty ten years earlier; by the end of the nineteenth century half of Boston was Irish.

The pattern became clear as Irish immigration mounted: they were country folk who were becoming city people. A nineteenth century English observer, Philip H. Bagenal, in describing the way in which the Irish settled right where they landed, said they had "blocked up the channels of immigration at the entrance, and remain like the sand which lies at the bar of a river mouth." Bagenal depicted the "descendants of the great Irish exodus of 1845–1848" as "tired migratory birds" that had fallen on America's eastern shores.

After landing in New York and Boston, the Irish were thrust into the depths of **tenement**[12] squalor. Even official accounts became overheated in describing their living conditions. A committee named by the New York State Assembly to investigate housing in New York [City] and Brooklyn reported in 1857 that its members "have witnessed, in their explorations, much calculated to shock the sensibilities and pain the heart. They have looked upon poverty in its nakedness, vice in its depravity."

---

[12] **tenement**—dwelling where poor families are housed close together.

Depicting the "condition of a great bulk of the foreigners daily landed at our wharves," the report found "these poor strangers, these immigrants . . . destitute, dispirited, sick, ignorant, abject."

The "most important phases" of the immigrant plight, reported the committee, "must be sought in crowded shanties and tenant-houses where newly-arrived shiploads are quartered upon already **domiciled**[13] 'cousins,' to share their 'bit and sup,' until such time as 'luck' may turn up or the entire colony go to the poor-house, or be carried off by fever or smallpox."

---

[13] **domiciled**—housed.

QUESTIONS TO CONSIDER

1. How did immigrants benefit from the conversion of Castle Garden?

2. What negative labels were attached to Irish immigrants? Was this a new experience for the Irish?

3. Why did American nativists detest Irish immigrants?

Charles Carroll An Irish Catholic hero of the American Revolution, Carroll was a signer of the Declaration of Independence.

Emigrants at Cork A prosperous Irish or Anglo-Irish family waits to board ship in this 1820 painting by Nathaniel Grogan.

Starving Poor children search for food in Cahera, Ireland, from an 1847 wood engraving. The very young and the very old were most susceptible to the twin famine plagues of starvation and disease. ▶

Mass Evictions More than 500,000 Irish people were evicted during the mass starvation, half of them by force. Under an 1847 law, tenants were not eligible for public assistance if they held more than a quarter acre of land. In order to be admitted to the workhouse, or to receive soup, they had to surrender their land and destroy their homes. ▼

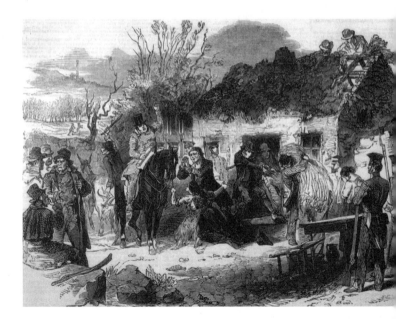

Economic Pressure Emigration began well before the Great Famine. Between 1800 and 1921, approximately seven and one-half million people left Ireland, easily the highest emigration rate in Europe. Most came to America. Ireland's population never recovered. Even today it is lower than during pre-Famine times.

▼

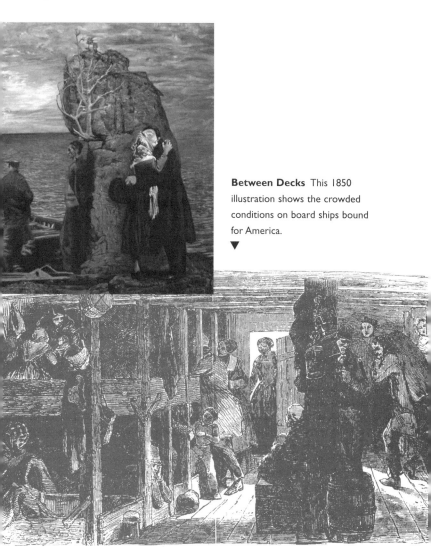

Between Decks This 1850 illustration shows the crowded conditions on board ships bound for America.

▼

▲

Arrival in New York This bigoted cartoon shows disagreeable-looking Irish emigrants arriving with only what they could carry.

Castle Garden Irish immigrants, along with Germans and others, came to this New York immigration center to receive medical inspections, exchange money, purchase tickets for further transportation, locate missing relatives, and look for jobs. It was replaced by Ellis Island in 1892.

▼

CHAPTER FOUR

Battlefield, Workplace, and Parish

Battling for Ireland and America

BY PAUL JONES

*Heroism in battle has been a time-honored theme of Irish history
and lore. Ireland's sons brought the tradition to America. Before
the Civil War (1861–1865), the 69th Regiment of the New York
State Militia had formed from groups of Irish volunteers who had
come together to train for the fight for Ireland's independence
from Britain. In fact, when a parade was held to honor the visiting
Prince of Wales, the 69th refused to march. Anti-immigrant groups
questioned Irish loyalty to America. But the Civil War silenced their
skepticism. The 69th Regiment, popularly known as "The Irish
Brigade," answered President Lincoln's call for militiamen. Fighting
under Irish and American flags, the 69th lost thirty-eight men in
the first major battle, Bull Run, with another fifty-nine wounded.
Of all the regiments the Union raised, the 69th ranked sixth in
casualties. The regiment fought in forty-eight major engagements
and paid for Irish acceptance in America with their lives. Historian
Paul Jones provides a glimpse of the 69th's heroism at the Battle
of Fredericksburg in 1862.*

This was the second year of the war, and tobacco was scarce in the North. Here [in Fredericksburg, Va.] there was plenty of it in warehouses or on barges, and men filled their **haversacks**.[1] During the hours of relative quiet after resistance ceased in the city (though the shelling continued from the heights), the Irish Brigade, like other units, quartered themselves in abandoned mansions and stores. Some found stocks of wine and liquors and supplies of ale. With tobacco for their clay pipes and a drink or two at hand, in the sure knowledge that the odds were against their seeing another sunset, the men passed the uneasy night. The more thoughtful wrote their names on bits of paper and pinned them to their coats, so they would not end up in an unmarked grave.

Next morning, when the regiments formed in the street, enterprising undertakers had their runners on the scene passing out business cards, guaranteeing prompt shipment home to all clients. The men in the ranks told them what they would do to them, if they had their feet free, and the officers drove them away. Then the Brigade marched to a position on the outskirts of the city, where a field hospital and a command post were set up. The route lay between sidewalks strewn with debris and broken furniture, and against a thin tide of early casualties. They remembered afterward a New York German in a wheelbarrow, with a **tourniquet**[2] on one shattered leg, dripping blood but puffing calmly on a **meerschaum**.[3]

It was a soft, damp, Irish kind of morning with a light fog. The thaw had held, and the footing was slippery. When the regiments came to parade rest, [Irish-born Union Brigadier General Thomas] Meagher and his staff inspected them; and the brigadier gave them encouraging words. His aides looked unusually serious; among them young [Robert] Emmet and their favorite

[1] **haversacks**—one-strap canvas bags soldiers wore over their shoulders.
[2] **tourniquet**—tight bandage.
[3] **meerschaum**—large, curved tobacco pipe.

Jack Gosson, not laughing for a change. To show the green, Meagher and his officers had put sprigs of box-wood in their hats. The men were allowed to break ranks, and every soldier in the Brigade came back to his place with a bit of evergreen on his cap.

Meagher's talk to each regiment was brief, reminding them that, because they were Irish, every eye would be upon them to see how they upheld a proud fighting tradition; and because they were Americans now, it was their duty and privilege to uphold the Union at any cost.

The flags were uncased, the Stars and Stripes and the green regimental banners with the golden harp and sunburst. As they went forward, the sun was barely visible through the hazy sky and the drifting smoke of black powder.

They came to the millstream that Burnside[4] had insisted wasn't there, and crossed it with difficulty on a narrow wooden bridge of which only the stringers remained intact. It was under fire from a Confederate battery, and the Brigade lost some men, before the others came under the protection of a slight fold in the ground. Here they threw off their blanket rolls and haversacks, preparing for action.

Ahead of them lay the rising slope of Marye's Heights, now one hundred and fifty yards away. They could see a field of stubble, then a snake fence and a small brick house, then another fence, and after that sixty yards of open land, running right up to a low stone wall at the crest of the hill. How the battle order stood in other parts of the fighting front was of no concern to them. This was the Brigade's objective, and it did not look easy. It looked worse than the sunken lane at Antietam.[5] French's division was to lead the way, and Hancock's would follow in support, if there was anything left to support. Units would attack in close order on a brigade front.

---

[4] Burnside—General Ambrose Burnside, commander of the Union forces at Fredericksburg.

[5] Antietam—the Battle of Antietam, fought earlier in 1862 near Sharpsburg, Maryland.

Waiting to go in, the men of the Irish Brigade had a preview of what they would face in a few minutes, as they watched the dozen regiments of French's division melt away in the furnace of fire on the slope below the stone wall. They knew they were good troops; they were old comrades from the days at Camp California. They saw them advance, scatter, rally again on their flags, claw their way forward for a few yards, and then fall back slowly. Zook's brigade of their own division went in next, but their gallant effort also faded in the hurricane of **grape**[6] and **canister**[7] from the Confederate artillery, and under the heavy volleys of musketry from two ranks of Rebels, firing in turn behind the stone wall.

"Irish Brigade, advance! Forward, double-quick, guide center!" Now they were for it, and they went in with a rush, across the withered stalks of a cornfield to the first fence, and beyond to the second fence, where they came fairly into the concentration of fire that blasted the final sixty yards.

Young Thomas F. Galwey, later associate editor of the *Catholic World* and professor at Manhattan College, was on the field that day. He had been in the first charge by French's division; and now, from the point where the remnants of his company had dug in, he watched the Irish Brigade. "Line after line of our men," he noted later in his diary, "advance in magnificent order out from the city towards us. But none of them pass the position which we took at our first dash and which we have continued to hold until now, in spite of the concentrated fire of the enemy's batteries, and the destructive **fusillade**[8] of his infantry.

"There is one exception, the Irish Brigade, which comes out from the city in glorious style, their green

---

[6] **grape**—(grapeshot), a cluster of small iron balls used as a cannon charge.

[7] **canister**—metal cylinder that, when fired from a gun, bursts and scatters the shot packed inside.

[8] **fusillade**—discharge of many firearms simultaneously.

sunbursts waving, as they have waved on many a bloody battlefield before, in the thickest of the fight where the grim and thankless butchery of war is done. Every man has a sprig of green in his cap, and a half-laughing, half-murderous look in his eye. They pass just to our left, poor fellows, poor, glorious fellows, shaking goodbye to us with their hats! They reach a point within a stone's throw of the stone wall. No farther. They try to go beyond, but are slaughtered. Nothing could advance further and live. They lie down doggedly, determined to hold the ground they have already taken. There, away out in the fields to the front and left of us, we see them for an hour or so, lying in line close to that terrible stone wall."

From the high ground behind the Confederate lines, General [Robert E.] Lee and his staff could see the whole panorama of battle, like a colorful pageant of flags and little toy soldiers. It was at this point that he turned to an aide, and said: "It is well that war is so frightful. Otherwise, we should become too fond of it."

[Confederate] General George Edward Pickett was there, too, and wrote his wife that his heart was wrung by the dauntless gallantry of the Irish attack on Marye's Heights. The correspondent of the London *Times*, by no means pro-Union, wrote his paper: "Never at Fontenoy, Albuera, or at Waterloo was more undaunted courage displayed by the sons of Erin[9] than during those six frantic dashes which they directed against the almost **impregnable**[10] position of their foe. . . . The bodies which lie in dense masses within forty yards of the muzzles of [Confederate] Colonel Walton's guns are the best evidence what manner of men they were who pressed on to death with the dauntlessness of a race which has gained glory on a thousand battlefields, and never more richly deserved it than at the foot of Marye's Heights on the 13th day of December, 1862."

---

[9] Erin—Ireland.

[10] **impregnable**—unable to be captured or entered by force.

At nightfall, the Brigade retired to the city, leaving its dead and wounded on the slope. Nearest the stone wall was the body of Major William Horgan of the 88th New York. The Confederates anticipated another attack, and their sharpshooters swept the slope so closely that it was impossible to stand upright without being hit. The casualties lay in great numbers on the field all of Sunday, the day following the battle; the Rebels had captured a copy of the order by Burnside in which he proposed to lead in person a fresh assault on Marye's Heights. He was out of his mind with grief and despair, and this time his staff and corps commanders firmly overruled him.

One of the few wounded brought in from the field under fire was Sergeant Sheridan of the 88th New York, who was in agony with a compound fracture of one leg. Four of his comrades crawled up the hill, hugging the ground, and Sergeant Slattery devised a new method of rescue, based on an Irish countryman's experience. "Boys," he said, "did yez ever see rats trying to get away with a goose egg? One rat lies down, the others roll the egg on top of him, he holds it in place with his four paws, and then they pull him and the egg off by his tail. Now, I'll lie down here on my back, you roll Sheridan on top of me, and I'll do my best to keep his leg even, while you pull on my feet." So they got Sheridan down, dragging Slattery like a sled, and taking most of the skin off his back.

At Fredericksburg, the Union lost over twelve thousand men, killed, wounded, and missing, against four thousand five hundred for the Confederates. It was a supremely depressing failure, after the victory at Antietam, where the Rebels lost almost fourteen thousand to twelve thousand three hundred and fifty on the Union side. The worst reflection, that sad Christmas, was that it had been totally unnecessary. The Union army was back where it started, having accomplished nothing in an attack from which nothing could have been expected except disaster. Burnside was foolish enough to blame his subordinates, and to attempt to have three of his generals dismissed from the service. The army knew better whose fault it was.

The losses of the Irish Brigade at Fredericksburg were heavy. Out of thirteen hundred men engaged, five hundred and forty-five were killed, wounded, or missing, presumed dead. At morning formation on the 14th, [Union] General [Winfield Scott] Hancock, looking over what remained of his shattered division, saw three privates of the Irish Brigade off by themselves on parade. "Damn it," he shouted, "you there, close up on your company!"

One of them saluted. "Sir, we *are* a company."

"The hell you say!" Even the superb Hancock was impressed. He returned the salute with extra care. "As you were!"

Little by little, the emergency dressing stations in Fredericksburg emptied. Ambulances took the wounded back over the pontoon bridges to the field hospitals at the permanent camp on Stafford Heights, where trains waited to take them to the great general hospitals in Washington, Baltimore, and Philadelphia.

QUESTIONS TO CONSIDER

1. What did the Irish Brigade gain by repeatedly charging the Confederates' safe position on Marye's Heights during the battle?

2. Why was it important for the officers and men of the 69th to "show the green" in their caps?

3. How did the actions of the Irish Brigade lead to the acceptance of Irish immigrants in America?

Photographing the Civil War

BY MARTIN W. SANDLER

Mathew Brady was born in 1823 in Warren County, New York, the son of immigrant parents from County Cork, Ireland. As a young man, he was fascinated with a new way to create fixed images of people and landscapes. He took a class in daguerreotype methods taught by Samuel F. B. Morse, the inventor of the telegraph, and acquired everything that was published on the subject. The young Irish American incorporated every new discovery and improvement into his studies, and he was soon able to produce pictures that were regarded as equal or superior to all that had been made before. He opened his first portrait gallery on Broadway in 1844 and almost overnight became New York's and America's leading daguerreotypist—even though he was only twenty-one years old. When the Civil War broke out, Brady mortgaged his New York studio and risked everything to capture the historic events in photographs. He said, "A spirit in my feet said 'go' and I went." His work, unlike anything seen before, provides a priceless view of the Civil War period, as explained here by historian Martin Sandler.

In the middle of the 1850s one person, more than any other, dominated the field of American photography. His name was Mathew B. Brady, and he was destined to become even more important and to rank with the most famous photographers of all time. Brady was one of a number of young photographers who received their training from Samuel F. B. Morse. He was a tireless worker who not only displayed a fine talent for taking photographs but also possessed a real business sense. In 1844, at the age of twenty-one, he opened his first **daguerreotype**[1] studio in New York. In that same year he was awarded first prize at the American Institute in New York for one of his daguerreotypes. It was the first of many gold medals and other awards he would win for his photography.

Brady's gallery was a tremendous success from the very beginning. The most famous people of his time came to his studio to be photographed. Among his early subjects were such celebrities as Daniel Webster, John Quincy Adams, and an aged Andrew Jackson. Brady's New York studio was so successful that in 1849 he opened another studio in Washington. This put him into even closer contact with the most important political figures of the day.

Brady was always searching for **innovations**[2] in photography. He was, for example, one of the first to perfect a method of handcoloring daguerreotypes. He spent years working on a publication he entitled *The Gallery of Illustrious Americans,* which included photographs and biographical sketches of leading personalities and was one of the first photographic books ever published.

Brady's business continued to grow to such an extent that by 1860 he had opened two new galleries in

---

[1] **daguerreotype**—early photographic process employing a light-sensitive, silver-coated metallic plate developed with mercury vapor.

[2] **innovations**—creative changes.

New York. Each was more elaborate than the previous one. In 1860 in his National Portrait Gallery in New York Brady took his most famous portrait. In the midst of the Lincoln-Douglas political debates, Abraham Lincoln arrived for a speech at the Cooper Union, a college in New York City. Accompanied by three members of the Young Men's Republican Committee, the candidate from Illinois went to Brady's gallery and had his portrait taken. After the important speech at the Cooper Union the next day, Brady's Lincoln portrait was in great demand. Thousands were sold and woodcuts were made from them for use in the leading news publications of the day. After Lincoln was elected President, he went to Brady's Washington studio for an inauguration portrait. While there, he stated, "Brady and the Cooper Union speech made me President."

Not long after Lincoln's inauguration, events took place that dramatically changed the course of the nation's history and the career of Mathew Brady. By 1861, the rift between North and South became **irreconcilable**,[3] and in April of that year the Civil War began. By this time Brady, like most American photographers, had abandoned the daguerreotype and was working exclusively with wet plates. He was convinced that he could organize teams of photographers, provide them with photographic wagons that could both carry the equipment they needed and serve as darkrooms in which to develop the wet plates, and take himself and his teams onto the battlefields.

Brady had many influential friends on both sides of the conflict. He used these contacts to gain the necessary permission to accompany the Union Army into the field. He was not concerned with the politics of the war. Brady's purpose was simple and clear—he was

---

[3] **irreconcilable**—impossible to resolve.

determined to become America's first battlefield photographer, the cameraman of the Civil War.

Between the time that war was declared and the first actual battle, Washington was a beehive of activity. Supplies were being gathered, troops were being trained, military strategy was being planned. Meanwhile, Brady's studio there was busier than ever before as thousands of soldiers made their way up its stairs to have *cartes de visite*[4] of themselves in uniform taken to be sent to loved ones at home. These photographs are important today for they reveal, among other things, the incredible youth of many soldiers in both armies. For Brady, this was a time in which all the logistics of putting teams of photographers into the field had to be completed. From January to April of 1862 he hired and trained the men who were to become America's first war photographers. Brady assigned these men to different territories in the war zones and arranged for the setting up of photographic bases in those areas.

There has always been controversy as to just how many of the dramatic Civil War photographs were taken by Brady himself. We know, for example, that Timothy O'Sullivan actually snapped the greatest number of pictures. Alexander Gardner took many others. We also know, however, that hundreds of the photographs *were* taken by Brady and that he was present at some of the most important battles of the war, coming close to injury or death on several occasions. In fact, he received his baptism under fire at the very first major engagement of the conflict—the Battle of Bull Run [in 1861].

Brady and his companions had two photographic wagons at Bull Run. They were specially designed to serve as darkrooms and had built-in shelves to hold chemicals, glass negatives, cameras, and other equipment. These photographic wagons soon became familiar

---

[4] *cartes de visite*—French term for calling cards, cards with one's name and address given when making visits.

sights at camps and battlefields throughout the war zones. The soldiers gave the wagons a name. "It's the Whatsit," they would shout whenever Brady or one of his fellow photographers arrived on the scene. Actually the "Whatsits" proved to be excellent targets for artillery blasts, and on more than one occasion Brady or one of the other members of the photographic team was lucky to escape with his life as shells exploded all around the wagon.

When the Battle of Bull Run began, Brady and his team of photographers immediately set up their cameras. There they took the first photographs of an American battlefield on the same day as the battle. The cameras of the time still did not allow for the capturing of action shots. But as soon as the firing stopped the photographers were on the field, recording dramatic images of the dead, the wounded—all the remnants of the historic skirmish.

The Battle of Bull Run was a disaster for the Union Army. Before it was over, most of the troops had turned and fled. Since the battle was fought close to Washington, Brady decided to return there with his wagon before setting out for the next theater of operation. Only a few hours after his return to the capital, word leaked out about the photographs he had taken. One newspaper proclaimed, "The public is indebted to Brady . . . for his excellent views of **grim-visaged**[5] war. He has been in Virginia with his camera and many and spirited are the pictures he has taken. His are the only records of the flight of Bull Run."

The Battle of Bull Run marked the beginning of American military photography. Throughout the rest of the war Brady, O'Sullivan, Gardner, and the other members of the photographic teams took picture after picture of every aspect of the war—soldiers in camp awaiting

---

[5] **grim-visaged**—having a terrible or forbidding face, a reference to a line from the opening scene of Shakespeare's *The Tragedy of King Richard the Third.*

battle, scenes at the battlefield moments after the firing had stopped, military hospitals and prisons, generals and privates, victors and vanquished. They risked the constant dangers of battle and worked under the most difficult conditions—freezing cold in the winters of 1862 and 1863 and burning heat in the summer of 1864.

By the middle of the war, Brady had more than thirty bases of operation. The photographs that were sent back to the Washington studio from the front had a tremendous impact upon the American public. Said one newspaper, "Mr. Brady has done something to bring home to us the terrible reality and earnestness of war. . . . Crowds of people are constantly going up the stairs [of his studio]. Follow them and you will find them bending over photographic views of the fearful battlefield, taken immediately after the action."

Brady, O'Sullivan, and the other combat photographers captured images of every phase of the conflict. Not only were photographs taken on land, but for the first time in American history, pictures of a navy at war were taken as well. During the early stages of the conflict, there were rather lengthy periods of quiet between battles. The war photographers used this time to take hundreds of pictures of soldiers and their officers in camp. The cameramen obviously were able to compose these camp pictures more carefully than their battlefield shots, and many of the photographs that resulted were truly outstanding. A photograph taken by Brady, for example, of three Union officers leaning against a tree reveals the photographer's expertise at composition and his sense of the dramatic.

A sense of the dramatic is also present in Alexander Gardner's photograph of President Abraham Lincoln visiting with General George McClellan and his staff at their field headquarters at Antietam in 1862. Lincoln, stovepipe hat and all, has been placed in the center of the photograph. The officers are posed facing him, all eyes supposedly riveted on the commander in chief. But as so often happened, the lure of the camera was too much for some of the men, and even in the presence of the President, they turned and stared into the lens.

QUESTIONS TO CONSIDER

1. When President Lincoln gave Brady and his photographs some of the credit for winning the election, the camera became a fixture of American politics. What role does the camera play in politics today?

2. How did Brady solve some of the logistical problems of Civil War photography?

3. Why do you think these first photographs of war had such an impact?

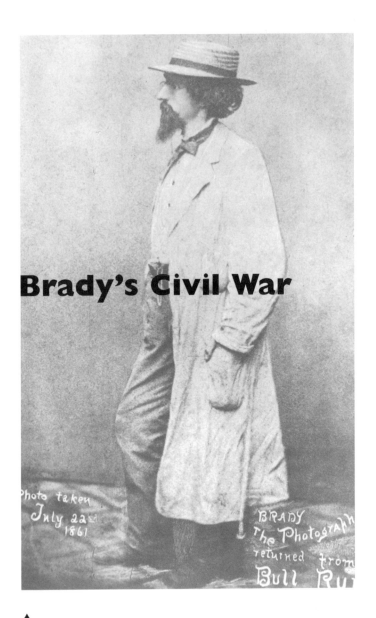

Brady's Civil War

Photo taken
July 22nd
1861

BRADY
The Photograph
returned from
Bull Ru

▲

War Photographer When the Civil War broke out, young Mathew Brady left his successful portrait studios in New York City and Washington, D.C., organized a team of twenty photographers, and produced a wealth of battlefield images.

▲

Wounded Union soldiers in the yard of the Marye house, Fredericksburg.

▲

Mass in the Field This photograph shows members of New York's all-Irish Union Army regiment, the Fighting 69th, gathered for mass.

No Irish Need Apply

BY KERBY MILLER AND PAUL WAGNER

Although most of the famine-era Irish immigrants were the sons and daughters of small farmers and agricultural workers, they were ill-equipped to become farmers themselves. They often arrived in America with few skills and no capital. Many were illiterate, and some spoke only the Irish language, Gaelic. Therefore, most could only find work at the bottom of the American economy: Irish women worked as servants, cooks, and millworkers; the men became miners, construction workers, lumbermen, dockhands, and ditch-diggers. They built the new nation's sewers, roads, streets, canals, and railroads, but not without encountering and enduring extreme prejudice and hatred because of their status as strangers and Roman Catholics. Historians Miller and Wagner review the problems of the immigrants in an excerpt from their book, Out of Ireland.

On a summer's night in 1855, Thomas McIntyre, a house-plasterer from County Tyrone in Ulster, sat down in his boarding house in Boston. Weary and sore from his day's labor, he wrote a letter to his sister back home in the village of Donemanagh.

August 27, 1855

Dear Sister,
I know today you are all, or at least a good part of you, at Donemanagh fair. I am just thinking as I sit here alone of the times I used to have on those occasions. But there are no Donemanagh fairs here. There is nothing here but work hard today and go to bed at night and rise and work harder tomorrow. Nothing but work work away.

John wants to know if I still play the fiddle any now, but you may tell him that if he was here to put on mortar for one week, he would have very little notion about fiddling on Saturday nights. I sometimes think, when I go to my room without any one to speak to me, of the nights when we used to sit down by the fire and draw down our old fiddles. My meditations are not very pleasant. However people need not expect a great deal of enjoyment when they come here.

Give my love to all my old neighbors and friends. You will scarce be able to make this hand-writing out—I was just beginning to think that I had the trowel[1] in my hand.

Farewell all,
T. McIntyre
Write soon.

Thomas McIntyre was one of many Irish immigrants who discovered to their sorrow that the streets of America were not paved with gold, but rather that the Irish immigrants were expected to pave the streets themselves—and for very low wages. The disillusioned letters that they wrote home could not stem the flood tide of Irish immigration, but they did spread a more balanced or realistic picture of life in the United States, informing would-be immigrants that America was not only a land of milk and honey—or of beef and whiskey,

---

[1] *trowel*—flat-bladed hand tool used for spreading mortar.

as Daniel Guiney had portrayed it. It was also what Irish country people came to perceive as a "land of sweat." In America, opportunities could be seized only by those who were able and willing to work much harder than they did at home—and willing to **forego**[2] many of the simple pleasures of Irish country life that McIntyre ruefully recalled.

If letters like McIntyre's were not sufficient warning, young Irish who still came to the United States with **naive**[3] illusions—"greenhorns" they were called by immigrants long-settled in America—soon learned some bitter truths.

"You must work or starve," the new arrivals were told. "This is not Ireland, this is America, and there is no bread for idlers here."

Poor pay and long hours of backbreaking toil were not the only conditions that Irish immigrants had to endure in the promised land, especially in the middle decades of the nineteenth century, when the Famine refugees arrived. As the historian Dennis Clark has commented, "Whether they were women servants or men who worked in steel mills, these were people who were subject to the most fierce **exploitation**[4] at a time when American capitalism had no governors and no **constraints**[5] upon it."

The exploitation of the Irish by Yankee American society was based on fundamental prejudice against them as human beings, not just as workers. As Dennis Clark further points out, "When the builders of canals wanted a labor force to build the Chesapeake Canal in Virginia, they went to the local plantation owners and said, 'Rent us your slaves.' But the planters replied, 'No

---

[2] **forego**—do without.

[3] **naive**—unsophisticated; simple.

[4] **exploitation**—utilization of another person for selfish purposes.

[5] **constraints**—restrictions, limits.

way, these slaves are worth money. Get Irishmen instead. If they die, there's no monetary loss."'

For the Famine immigrants, especially, exploitation began as soon as they set foot on American shores. When they arrived, many Irish immigrants quickly learned that American seaports were inhabited by what they called "Yankee tricksters," who infested the docklands and tried to rob the unwary Irish of their little capital or possessions. Those who escaped the human sharks of New York City, New Orleans, and other ports soon discovered that their new American employers and foremen were often as harsh and unsympathetic as their old landlords in Ireland.

For instance, as Patrick Walsh from County Cork later remembered:

In the years 1851–52, the Troy and Boston railroad was being made through the north-eastern part of the State of New York. The contractors and others concerned advertised liberally, promised the finest terms to the working men, in order to bring together the greatest number. They came from far distances, and without the means of returning in case of disappointment. Accordingly, when the contractors found they had enough, and to spare, of laboring hands, they reduced the wages and kept on reducing until they brought it down to 55 cents a day. Against this rate the men went out on strike, as it would not support them, and matters began to wear a threatening aspect. At length, the legal authorities were called upon, with military force, to drive them off (which is always the custom in such cases).

I went to see the condition of those that remained, and in their "shanties," with the fierce wind howling through them, a scene of suffering presented itself which made the heart sick. All along for miles was one continued scene of anguish and suffering, as if some peculiar curse was chasing the unfortunate people of Ireland. Yet these things were noticed as mere items of news in the papers, without any comment, as no concern was felt in their case, being Irish.

Incidents such as Patrick Walsh described were not uncommon. Often the wages of Irish miners and laborers on canal, railroad, and building sites were paid in overpriced goods, in devalued currency, or sometimes not at all. The injustices of the company stores and crooked scales in the Pennsylvania coal mining camps of the 1870s unleashed the fury of the Molly Maguires. This group of immigrant workers from the west of Ireland was named for an anti-landlord movement operating there.

Similarly, in 1859 Irish laborers in Jersey City barricaded the railroad tracks they had just constructed to protest not receiving their promised wages. In return, the city's business leaders and press condemned them as "animals" and as a "**mongrel**[6] mass of ignorance and crime and superstition" who were "utterly unfit for the common courtesies and decencies of life." After a massive show of military force, six of the Irish workers received two-year prison terms for their affront to "order" and the "sacred rights of property."

As another immigrant put it more bluntly than had Patrick Walsh, the life of an Irish laborer in mid-nineteenth century America was often "despicable, humiliating, and slavish." There was "no love for him, no protection of life. He can be shot down, run through, kicked, cuffed, spat on—and no **redress**,[7] but a response of 'Serves the [ethnic epithet] right, damn him.'"

Irish immigrants experienced such treatment and prejudice from native-born Americans only in part because they were impoverished, unskilled foreigners. They were hated because they were Irish and because they were Catholic.

Most Americans prided themselves on both their British ancestry and their Protestantism. They also believed that Irish poverty was a sign of laziness and immorality, of ignorance and superstition—traits they considered inseparable from Irishness and Catholicism.

---

[6] **mongrel**—like animals of mixed breeds or species.

[7] **redress**—way to set right, remedy, or rectify.

Indeed, in the nineteenth century many Protestant Americans were convinced that the Catholic Church itself was the sworn enemy of America's democratic institutions, and they feared that the Irish immigrants represented the advance army of **papal**[8] aggression. Poor immigrants were not the only victims of Yankee, or **nativist**,[9] prejudices, as John Blake Dillon, an Irish-born lawyer in New York City, complained bitterly, "The great majority of the American people are, in heart and soul, anti-Catholic, but more especially anti-Irish. Everything Irish is **repugnant**[10] to them."

Because of such beliefs, the newspapers in New York, Boston, and elsewhere often depicted the Irish as violent and drunken, even as subhumans more akin to apes than to native-born Americans. Some employers refused to hire Irish Catholics and advertised for workers with the warning notice, "No Irish Need Apply." And, when Irish laborers did find work, their employers, foremen, and even their non-Irish fellow workers often treated them in what Patrick Taggart, a carpenter from County Mayo, called "an insulting manner," with "**scurrilous**[11] attacks on our **creed**[12] and country." Even Irish Americans who overcame poverty and prejudice, such as James Michael Curley, many times mayor of Boston and once governor of Massachusetts, were rarely allowed to forget what Curley had learned as a poor, Irish-speaking boy in the slums of Roxbury. They "belonged to an Irish Catholic minority who were despised socially and discriminated against politically."

On more than a few occasions, anti-Irish Catholic prejudices exploded into violence, sometimes with fatal results. In 1837 a mob of Protestant workmen from Boston burned

---

[8] **papal**—concerning the pope, the leader of the Roman Catholic Church.
[9] **nativist**—advocate of a political philosophy that favors the interest of established citizens over those of immigrants.
[10] **repugnant**—offensive, distasteful, or repulsive.
[11] **scurrilous**—foul-mouthed, outrageous.
[12] **creed**—statement of religious belief.

to the ground a Catholic convent in nearby Charlestown. In 1844 native-born Americans in Philadelphia rioted for a week, destroying many Catholic churches and much of the Irish neighborhood in the north of the city and killing at least a dozen immigrants. "The people here think as little of killing others as you would of killing the mice in a cornstack," wrote one frightened immigrant.

The large numbers and impoverished status of the famine immigrants began to horrify many Protestant Americans. In the 1850s nativism became a nationwide political movement in the form of the "Know-Nothing" or Native American Party. The Know-Nothings controlled several state governments, where they passed punitive anti-Catholic and anti-immigrant legislation, and they seemed capable of winning control of Congress and the White House. Some Irish immigrants sadly concluded that the Penal Laws were on the verge of re-enactment, not in Ireland, but in the "Land of Liberty."

In 1855 James Dixon, an Irish seaman in Philadelphia, wrote a letter to his sister who lived in County Wexford . . . warning his former neighbors not to emigrate to America:

September 4, 1855

Dear Catherine,
I hope the prospects in Ireland are good this year, respecting the crops I mean. I suppose the taxes will be increased to crush the poor people yet. However, if people can live comfortably in Ireland they ought to remain there, for affairs are becoming fearful in this country. The Know-Nothings have murdered a number of Irishmen in Louisville and destroyed their property. And if feelings continue as they are, on the increase, an Irishman will not get to live in this country. Even if people are poor in Ireland, at least they will be protected from murderers. I remain,

Your affectionate brother,
James Dixon

The Know-Nothing threat faded in the late 1850s, and Irish-Americans' loyalty to the Union and their participation in the Civil War served to calm the fears of many Yankees. Indeed, Dixon himself moved to California, where eventually he became a wealthy rancher—as well as the lover of the wife of a British nobleman!—in Marin County, north of San Francisco. Despite Irish Catholics' economic successes and wartime sacrifices, **aversion**[13] to Irish immigrants and their religion remained common among Protestant Americans throughout the rest of the nineteenth century—and even into the twentieth.

For many decades, being Irish and Catholic was still a **stigma**[14] in American society, and prejudice continued to **thwart**[15] the ambitions of middle-class as well as working-class Irish-Americans. In the 1890s the members of a new and temporarily powerful nativist organization, the American Protective Association, pledged to refuse to vote for or even to work and associate with Irish-American Catholics. During World War I, President Woodrow Wilson (himself the descendant of Orangemen[16] from Ulster) and other pro-British Americans were deeply suspicious of Irish- American loyalties, fearing that ancient Irish animosities against England might cause the immigrants and their children to side with Germany. In the 1920s a resurgent Ku Klux Klan attacked Irish Catholics as well as Jewish and African Americans. And in 1928 the first Irish Catholic candidate for President of the United States, New York's Al Smith, was defeated in part because of such prejudice. . . .

---

[13] **aversion**—intense dislike.

[14] **stigma**—mark of low status. Originally it was a mark burned into the skin of a criminal or slave.

[15] **thwart**—prevent from taking place.

[16] Orangemen—Protestants from Northern Ireland; originally those who supported William of Orange, the Protestant English king who defeated a Catholic army at the critical Battle of the Boyne in Ireland in 1690.

QUESTIONS TO CONSIDER

1. Why did the nativists and Know-Nothing Party members hate and fear the immigrant Irish?

2. What were some of the characteristics of the fierce exploitation of nineteenth-century labor?

3. In what ways might newly arrived immigrants today face the same sort of discrimination the Irish faced?

The Molly Maguires Vindicated (Assuming They Existed)

BY WILLIAM D. GRIFFIN

In the mid-nineteenth century, thousands of Irish Famine refugees migrated to the anthracite coal region of Schuylkill County, Pennsylvania. The working and living conditions they found were almost as bad as the ones they had left behind in Ireland. Workers lived on company-owned property, in three-room shanties often housing twenty people or more. All male members of the family, including those as young as seven years old, worked in the mine. The mining families were forced to buy all their food at the company store, and credit was deducted from their pay envelopes. The Coal and Iron Police, who owed their loyalty and jobs to the company, kept order according to company policies. Mine owners resisted trade unionism, often violently. Author William D. Griffin recalls the tragedy of the Molly Maguires in this excerpt from The Book of Irish Americans.

Like so many other negative images of the Irish-American, the Molly Maguires have received a great deal of publicity. From a novel by Conan Doyle[1] *(The Valley of Fear)* to a Hollywood melodrama starring Sean Connery and Richard Harris, they have entered the popular imagination as a ruthless band of criminals, carrying out a reign of terror in the Pennsylvania coalfields. Few are aware, however, of their **exoneration**[2] a century after their downfall. And some still insist that there never was such an organization.

According to standard encyclopedia accounts, the Molly Maguires were an anti-landlord secret society formed in Ireland during the early nineteenth century and imported to America by the 1850s. The origin of the name is variously **ascribed**.[3] According to some, Molly Maguire was a heroic woman who resisted oppressive landlords during the eighteenth century. Other accounts maintain that the members wore female clothes during their terrorist attacks to disguise their identity. The organization is said to have developed among coal miners in Pennsylvania as an offshoot of the Ancient Order of Hibernians.[4] The Mollies expanded rapidly after the Civil War and carried out acts of violence, arson, and **sabotage**[5] against mine owners, supervisors, and informers. A massive strike in the Pennsylvania coalfields in 1875 was attributed to them. A detective, the Irish-born James McParlan, infiltrated the society, won the confidence of its leaders, and handed them over to the authorities. Twenty of the Mollies were convicted of murder and executed,[6] and by 1878 the society was no more.

---

[1] Conan Doyle—Sir Arthur Conan Doyle, an Irish Catholic by birth, became famous as an English mystery writer and the creator of Sherlock Holmes.

[2] **exoneration**—freeing from a charge; declaration of blamelessness.

[3] **ascribed**—associated, attributed.

[4] Ancient Order of Hibernians—an Irish-American fraternal society.

[5] **sabotage**—damaging property or machinery in order to obstruct production.

[6] All of the men executed were Irish by birth or descent. All were Catholics and all were members of the Ancient Order of Hibernians (AOH).

But some deny that it ever existed. Certain labor historians contend that the Molly Maguires were invented out of thin air by the mine bosses who wanted to destroy the workers' leadership and their will to resist. The men who were executed, these historians declare, were "framed" by perjured testimony and convicted by juries that systematically excluded Irishmen. In this view, the men who died as "Molly Maguire murderers" were martyrs of the American labor movement, the **precursors**[7] of the United Mine Workers Union that came into existence some years later.

Historians of the Ancient Order of Hibernians, while sometimes casting doubt on the very existence of the Mollies, are chiefly concerned to show that it was not synonymous with the AOH. One writer held that the Mollies were wolves in sheep's clothing who joined the AOH to cover up their criminal activities. Another suggests that the men who were hanged were simply the victims of anti-Irish prejudice and that their membership in the AOH—an innocent organization—singled them out for persecution. Such commentators reject McParlan's testimony that the AOH and the Molly Maguires were one and the same. Whatever the truth, John Kehoe, the alleged leader of the Mollies, was a senior official of the AOH, and four others of those hanged were AOH divisional officers or county delegates.

In December 1978, just a few days after the one hundredth anniversary of John Kehoe's death, his great-grandson petitioned the Pennsylvania Board of Pardons to "remove the stigma that hangs over my family." His argument for reversal of sentence was **buttressed**[8] with **ample**[9] testimony by historians and lawyers. A month later, the governor of Pennsylvania signed a posthumous pardon for Jack Kehoe. Speaking to reporters,

---

[7] **precursors**—forerunners.

[8] **buttressed**—bolstered or reinforced.

[9] **ample**—abundant.

the governor declared: "We can be proud of the men known as the Molly Maguires because they defiantly faced allegations that made trade unionism a criminal conspiracy. These men gave their lives on behalf of the labor struggle."

Thus the Molly Maguires have been vindicated—even if they never existed.

QUESTIONS TO CONSIDER

1. What difference, if any, does it make whether or not the Pennsylvania Molly Maguires ever existed?

2. Why might the Ancient Order of Hibernians want to distance itself from the Mollies, as author Griffin suggests?

3. What is the significance of the governor's pardon?

Songs of Irish Assimilation

Music has been a vital ingredient in the culture of Ireland and other remaining Celtic areas of the world—Scotland, Wales, the Brittanny section of France, and the Galicia region of northeastern Spain—since before history was first recorded. In ancient Ireland, both historic deeds and folk tales were passed from generation to generation by traveling singers called "bards"—a name that since has been applied to such writers and poets as William Shakespeare, whose England once was also a Celtic land. The tradition of story-telling through music came with the Irish immigrants to America, as the following three songs illustrate. Each deals with the difficult lives of nineteenth century Irish Americans—lives often as tough as those of the families they left behind in Ireland.

No Irish Need Apply

ANONYMOUS

I'm a decent boy just landed from the town of Ballyfad;
I want a situation and I want it very bad.
I've seen employment advertised, "It's just the thing,"
    says I.
But the dirty spalpeen[1] ended with "No Irish Need
    Apply."
"Whoo," says I, "that is an insult, but to get the place I'll
    try. I'll try,
"So I went there to see the blackguard[2] with his "No
    Irish Need Apply."

Chorus:
   Some do think it is a misfortune to be christened
            Pat or Dan,
   But to me it is an honor to be born an Irishman.

I started out to find the house, I got there mighty soon;
I found the old chap seated—he was reading
    the Tribune.
 I told him what I came for, when he in a rage did fly;
"No!" he says, "You are a Paddy,[3] and no Irish need
    apply."
Then I gets my dander[4] rising, and I'd like to black his
    eye
For to tell an Irish gentleman "No Irish Need Apply."

Chorus Repeat

---

[1] spalpeen—ad for a landless laborer.

[2] blackguard—scoundrel.

[3] Paddy—Irishman; Paddy is the nickname for Padraic, the Irish language word
for Patrick.

[4] dander—temper.

I couldn't stand it longer so a-hold of him I took,
And I gave him such a welting[5] as he'd get at
Donnybrook.[6]
He hollered "Milia Murther,"[7] and to get away did try,
And swore he'd never write again "No Irish Need
Apply."
Well, he made a big apology; I told him then goodbye,
Saying, "When next you want a beating, write 'No Irish
Need Apply.'"

Chorus Repeat

Paddy on the Railway

ANONYMOUS

In eighteen hundred and forty-one
I put me corduroy breeches on
I put me corduroy breeches on
To work upon the railway.

Chorus:
> Filli-me-cori-oori-ay
> Filli-me-cori-oori-ay
> Filli-me-cori-oori-ay
> To work upon the railway.

In eighteen hundred and forty-two
I left the Old World for the New,
Bad cess[8] to the luck that brought me through
To work upon the railway.

---

[5] welting—beating that raises welts.
[6] Donnybrook—suburb of Dublin. The fair at Donnybrook is noted for its brawls.
[7] "Milia Murther"—"ghastly murder."
[8] cess—fortune or fate, in Gaelic.

Chorus Repeat

In eighteen hundred and forty-three
'Twas then that I met sweet Biddy McGee.
An elegant wife she's been to me
While working on the railway.

Chorus Repeat

In eighteen hundred and forty-four
I traveled the land from shore to shore,
I traveled the land from shore to shore
To work upon the railway.

Chorus Repeat

In eighteen hundred and forty-five
I found myself more dead than alive.
I found myself more dead than alive
from working on the railway.

Chorus Repeat

It's "Pat do this"
and "Pat do that,"
Without a stocking or cravat,[9]
Nothing but an old straw hat
While I worked on the railway.

Chorus Repeat

In eighteen hundred and forty-seven
Sweet Biddy McGee, she went to heaven;
If she left one kid she left eleven,
To work upon the railway.

---

[9] cravat—necktie.

Kilkelly

BY PETER JONES AND STEVE JONES

Kilkelly, Ireland 18 and 60, my dear and loving son John,
Your good friend the schoolmaster, Pat McNamara, was
    so good to write
Your brothers have all gone to find work in England,
    the house is so empty and sad
The crop of potatoes is sorely infected, a third to a half
    of them bad
And your sister Bridgett and Patrick O'Donnell are
    going to be married in June
Your mother says not to work on the railroad; be sure
    to come home soon

Kilkelly, Ireland 18 and 70, my dear and loving son John
Hello to your missus and to your four children and
    may they grow healthy and strong
Michael has got in a wee bit of trouble, I guess that he
    never will learn
Because of the dampness there's no turf to speak of and
    now we have nothing to burn
Bridgett is happy and name a child for her although
    she's got six of her own
You say you found work but you don't say what kind
    or when you'll be coming home

Kilkelly, Ireland 18 and 80, my dear sons Michael and John

I'm sorry to give you the very sad news that our dear old mother has gone

We buried her down at the church in Kilkelly, your brothers and Bridgett were there

You don't have to worry, she died very quickly, remember her in your prayers

And it's so good to hear that Michael's returning with money he's sure to find land

For the crops have been poor and the people are selling, any price they can

Kilkelly, Ireland 18 and 90, my dear and loving son John

I suppose that I must be close on 80 but it's 30 years since you've gone

Because of all that money you sent me I'm still living out on my own

Michael has built himself a fine house and Bridgett's daughters are grown

Thank you for sending your family picture, they're lovely young women and men

You say you might come for a visit, what joy to see you again

Kilkelly, Ireland 18 and 92, my dear brother John
I'm sorry I didn't write sooner to tell you that Father
  has passed on
He was living with Bridgett, she says he was cheerful
  and healthy right down to the end,
Why you should have seen him with the grandchildren,
  and Pat McNamara your friend
We buried him along side of Mother down at the
  Kilkelly church-yard
He was a strong and feisty old man considering his life
  was so hard
And it's funny the way he kept talking about you and
  called for you at the end
Oh why don't you think about coming to visit, we'd
  love to see you again.

QUESTIONS TO CONSIDER

1. How would you characterize the mood expressed in "No Irish Need Apply"? Why do you think people would have enjoyed singing it?

2. How does the singer's description of himself as "a decent boy" and "an Irish gentleman" make his use of violence seem out of character or humorous?

3. In what ways does *Paddy on the Railway* seem to define an Irishman's life by his work? How does the song differ from a plantation slave work song?

4. What is the main point of "Kilkelly"?

Poor Children, Hard Labor

BY MARY HARRIS "MOTHER" JONES

Mary Harris Jones—who became an American labor leader and social critic—was born into a poor family in Cork, Ireland, in 1830. Her father, a laborer, came to America five years later and then sent for his family. When young, Jones worked as a seamstress and a school-teacher, but her life was to be marked by tragedy and suffering. A yellow fever epidemic in Memphis in 1867 killed her husband, an iron worker, and her four children. Once they were buried, Jones nursed other sufferers until the plague ended. She returned to Chicago, where she previously owned a dressmaking shop, and opened another. But in 1871 she was made homeless when the great Chicago fire burned her establishment. While living in St. Mary's Church, she began to attend meetings of the Knights of Labor. She ultimately became a union organizer for the United Mineworkers of America, and—nicknamed "Mother Jones" by admirers—spent the rest of her life as a tireless advocate for working people. Her investigation of the exploitation of poor children is from her Autobiography of Mother Jones.

When the railroad workers' strike ended I went down to Cottondale [Alabama] to get a job in the cotton mills.

I wanted to see for myself if the gruesome stories of little children working in the mills were true.

I applied for a job but the manager told me he had nothing for me unless I had a family that would work also. I told the manager I was going to move my family to Cottondale but I had come on ahead to see what chances there were for getting work.

"Have you children?"

"Yes, there are six of us."

"Fine," he said. He was so enthusiastic that he went with me to find a house to rent.

"Here's a house that will do plenty," said he. The house he brought me to was a sort of two-story plank shanty. The windows were broken and the door sagged open. Its latch was broken. It had one room downstairs and an unfinished loft upstairs. Through the cracks in the roof the rain had come in and rotted the flooring. Downstairs there was a big old open fireplace in front of which were holes big enough to drop a brick through.

The manager was delighted with the house.

* * *

I took the house, promising to send for my family by the end of the month when they could get things wound up on the farm. I was given work in the factory, and there I saw the children, little children working, the most heartrending* spectacle in all life. Sometimes it seemed to me I could not look at those silent little figures; that I must go north, to the grim coal fields, to the Rocky Mountain camps, where the labor fight is at least fought by grown men.

Little girls and boys, barefooted, walked up and down between the endless rows of spindles, reaching thin little hands into the machinery to repair snapped threads. They crawled under machinery to oil it. They replaced spindles all day long, all day long; night through, night through. Tiny babies of six years old with faces of sixty did an eight-hour shift for ten cents a day. If they fell asleep, cold water was dashed in their faces, and the voice of the manager yelled above the ceaseless racket and whir of the machines.

* * *

At five-thirty in the morning, long lines of little grey children came out of the early dawn into the factory, into the maddening noise, into the lint filled rooms. Outside the birds sang and the blue sky shone. At the lunch half-hour, the children would fall to sleep over their lunch of cornbread and fat pork. They would lie on the bare floor and sleep. Sleep was their recreation, their release, as play is to the free child. . . .

* * *

But they had Sundays, for the mill owners, and the mill folks themselves were **pious**.[1] To Sunday School went the babies of the mills, there to hear how God had inspired the mill owner to come down and build the mill, so as to give His little ones work that they might develop into industrious, patriotic citizens and earn money to give to the missionaries to convert the poor unfortunate **heathen**[2] Chinese.

My "six children" not arriving, the manager got suspicious of me so I left Cottondale and went to Tuscaloosa where I got work in a rope factory. This factory was run also by child labor. Here, too, were the children running up and down between spindles. The lint was heavy in the room. The machinery needed constant cleaning. The tiny, slender bodies of the little children crawled in and about under dangerous machinery, oiling and cleaning. Often their hands were crushed. A finger was snapped off.

* * *

In the morning I went off shift with the little children. They stumbled out of the heated atmosphere of the

---

[1] **pious**—religious.
[2] **heathen**—not Christian.

mill, shaking with cold as they came outside. They passed on their way home the long grey line of little children with their dinner pails coming in for the day's shift.

They die of pneumonia, these little ones, of bronchitis and **consumption**.[3] But the birth rate like the dividends is large and another little hand is ready to tie the snapped threads when a child worker dies.

I went from Tuscaloosa to Selma, Alabama, and got a job in a mill. I boarded with a woman who had a dear little girl of eleven years working in the same mill with me.

On Sunday a group of mill children were going out to the woods. They came for Maggie. She was still sleeping and her mother went into the tiny bedroom to call her.

"Get up, Maggie, the children are here for you to go to the woods."

"Oh, mother," she said, "just let me sleep; that's lots more fun. I'm so tired. I just want to sleep forever."

So her mother let her sleep.

The next day she went as usual to the mill. That evening at four o'clock they brought her home and laid her tiny body on the kitchen table. She was asleep— forever. Her hair had caught in the machinery and torn her scalp off.

At night after the day shift came off work, they came to look at their little companion. A solemn line of little folks with old, old faces, with thin round shoulders, passed before the corpse, crying. They were just little children but death to them was a familiar figure.

"Oh, Maggie," they said, "We wish you'd come back. We're so sorry you got hurted!"

I did not join them in their wish. Maggie was so tired and she just wanted to sleep forever.

I did not stay long in one place. As soon as one showed interest in or sympathy for the children, she was suspected, and laid off. Then, too, the jobs went to grown-ups that could bring children. I left Alabama for South Carolina, working in many mills.

---

[3] **consumption**—tuberculosis.

In one mill, I got a day-shift job. On my way to work I met a woman coming home from night work. She had a tiny bundle of a baby in her arms.

"How old is the baby?"

"Three days. I just went back this morning. The boss was good and saved my place."

"When did you leave?"

"The boss was good; he let me off early the night the baby was born."

"What do you do with the baby while you work?"

"Oh, the boss is good and he lets me have a little box with a pillow in it beside the loom. The baby sleeps there and when it cries, I nurse it."

So this baby, like hundreds of others, listened to the whiz and whir of machinery before it came into the world. From its first weeks, it heard the **incessant**[4] racket raining down upon its ears, like iron rain. It crawled upon the linty floor. It toddled between forests of spindles. In a few brief years it took its place in the line. It renounced childhood and childish things and became a man of six, a wage earner, a snuff sniffer, a personage upon whose young-old shoulders fortunes were built.

And who is responsible for this appalling child slavery? Everyone. Alabama passed a child labor law, **endeavoring**[5] to some extent to protect its children. And Northern capitalists from Massachusetts and Rhode Island defeated the law. Whenever a Southern state attempts reform, the mill owners, who are for the most part Northerners, threaten to close the mills. They reach legislatures, they send lobbies to work against child labor reform, and money, Northern money for the most part, secures the **nullification**[6] of reform laws through control of the courts.

The child labor reports of the period in which I made this study put the number of children under fourteen years of age working in mills as fully 25 per cent of the

---

[4] **incessant**—never stopping; continual.

[5] **endeavoring**—making an earnest attempt; trying.

[6] **nullification**—cancellation.

workers; working for a **pittance**,[7] for eight, nine, ten hours a day, a night. And mill owners declared dividends ranging from 50 per cent to 90.

* * *

From the South, burdened with the terrible things I had seen, I came to New York and held several meetings to make known conditions as I had found them. I met the opposition of the press and of capital. For a long time after my Southern experience, I could scarcely eat. Not alone my clothes, but my food, too, at times seemed bought with the price of the toil of children. . . .

Anyway, during those months, I came into intimate contact with the miners and their families. I went through every mine from Pittsburgh to Brownsville. Mining at its best is wretched work, and the life and surroundings of the miner are hard and ugly. His work is down in the black depths of the earth. He works alone in a drift. There can be little friendly companionship as there is in the factory; as there is among men who built bridges and houses, working together in groups. The work is dirty. Coal dust grinds itself into the skin, never to be removed. The miner must stoop as he works in the drift. He becomes bent like a gnome.

His work is utterly fatiguing. Muscles and bones ache. His lungs breathe coal dust and the strange, damp air of places that are never filled with sunlight. His house is a poor makeshift and there is little to encourage him to make it attractive. The company owns the ground it stands on, and the miner feels the **precariousness**[8] of his hold. Around his house is mud and slush. Great mounds of **culm**,[9] black and sullen, surround him. His children are perpetually grimy from play on the culm mounds. The wife struggles with dirt, with inadequate water supply, with small wages, with overcrowded shacks.

---

[7] **pittance**—very small salary.

[8] **precariousness**—uncertainty, instability.

[9] **culm**—coal dust.

The miner's wife, who in the majority of cases, worked from childhood in the near-by silk mills, is over-burdened with child bearing. She ages young. She knows much illness. Many a time I have been in a home where the poor wife was sick in bed, the children crawling over her, quarreling and playing in the room, often the only warm room in the house.

* * *

I got to know the life of the breaker boys. The coal was hoisted to a **cupola**[10] where it was ground. It then came rattling down in chutes, beside which, ladder-wise, sat little breaker boys whose job it was to pick out the slate from the coal as the black rivers flowed by. Ladders and ladders of little boys sat in the gloom of the breakers, the dust from the coal swirling continuously up in their faces. To see the slate they must bend over their task. Their shoulders were round. Their chests narrow.

A breaker boss watched the boys. He had a long stick to strike the knuckles of any lad seen neglecting his work. The fingers of the little boys bled, bled on to the coal. Their nails were cut to the quick.

A labor certificate was easy to get. All one had to do was to swear to a notary for twenty-five cents that the child was the required age.

The breaker boys were not Little Lord Fauntleroys.[11] Small chaps smoked and chewed and swore. They did men's work and they had men's ways, men's vices and men's pleasures. They fought and spit tobacco and told stories out on the culm piles on a Sunday. They joined the breaker boys' union and beat up **scabs**.[12] They refused to let their little brothers and sisters go to school if the children of scabs went.

---

[10] **cupola**—circular furnace used in the mining process.

[11] Little Lord Fauntleroys—a reference to a fictional character in a nineteenth-century English novel who was a young boy raised as a pampered aristocrat.

[12] **scabs**—nonunion workers, sometimes used by management to break strikes by union members.

In many mines I met the trapper boys. Little chaps who open the door for the mule when it comes in for the coal and who close the door after the mule has gone out. Runners and helpers about the mine. . . .

I met a little trapper boy one day. He was so small that his dinner bucket dragged on the ground.

"How old are you, lad?" I asked him.

". . .I'm ten come Christmas."

"Why don't you go to school?"

"Gee," he said—though it was really something stronger—"I ain't lost no leg!" He looked proudly at his little legs.

I knew what he meant: that lads went to school when they were incapacitated by accidents.

Through the ceaseless efforts of the unions, through continual agitation, we have done away with the most outstanding evils of child labor in the mines. Pennsylvania has passed better and better laws. More and more children are going to school. Better schools have come to the mining districts. We have yet a long way to go. Fourteen years of age is still too young to begin the life of the breaker boy. There is still too little joy and beauty in the miner's life, but one who like myself has watched the long, long struggle knows that the end is not yet.

QUESTIONS TO CONSIDER

1. Why does Jones have to lie about having children?

2. Why do the children make "good" employees for the mill?

3. Why does Jones say that everyone is responsible for child slavery?

The Parish: The Building of Community

BY TERRY GOLWAY

After 1820, Irish immigrants identified with the Catholic Church to such an extent that an attack on one was seen as an attack on the other. As journalist Terry Golway explains in this excerpt from The Irish in America, *the Catholic parish provided a haven of shared values and rituals for those Irish seeking refuge from the trauma of the melting pot. In a sense, the parish represented the Ireland that immigrants left behind. No hostile or offensive customs could penetrate the parish, and the children of Irish-born parents grew up together and married in the same church in which they were baptized.*

Like so many other aspects of Irish-American life, the relationship between immigrant and parish changed with the coming of the famine immigrants. Until the late 1840s and early 1850s, Irish Catholics in America were not particularly churchgoing. Weekly mass attendance before the famine has been estimated at about 40 percent, a number that doesn't suggest images of a devout and pious people. No doubt mass attendance would have been higher were there more churches, more parishes, and more priests. But the Catholic Church in America before the famine was low in numbers, money, and priest power. There were ten churches to serve New York's ninety thousand Catholics in 1840, while Philadelphia had twelve parishes and Boston had nine in 1850. The head of the Church in New York, Archbishop John Hughes, an immigrant from County Tyrone who started life in America as a gardener, complained that "the insufficient number of churches has been . . . an immense drawback on the progress of religion."

The famine immigrants and those who came afterward provided, in spite of their terrible poverty, the means and numbers for an astonishing expansion of parish life in America. The number of parishes in Philadelphia doubled between 1850 and 1860. Growth was somewhat slower, but still astonishing in New York, where the number of parishes doubled between 1845 and 1863, and in Boston, which saw 100 percent growth between 1850 and 1870. Many of the new **congregants**[1] who escaped starvation in Ireland believed that their suffering was a judgment from on high, an analysis that Charles Trevelyan, who was in charge of Britain's relief operations, hoped the Irish Catholic clergy communicated to their hungry and dying congregations. The "poor people," he wrote, should not be "deprived of knowing that they are suffering from an affliction of God's providence."

In post-famine Ireland itself, with a rural society and its customs and traditions wiped out, the Catholic Church was all the poor Irish had left, and from the

---

[1] **congregants**—members of a church's congregation or parish.

suffering and hunger rose what historian Emmet Larkin called a "devotional revolution." Mass attendance tripled in the post-famine period. **Vocations**[2] to the priesthood and convent also grew, and from those ranks would come the Irish priests and nuns who would dominate the American parish. (More than fifteen hundred priests were dispatched to America from a single Dublin seminary in the late nineteenth century.) In place of the **decimated**[3] institutions of village life, the post-famine Irish parish offered all manner of societies, groups, and rituals intended to inspire a richer (and more disciplined) faith as well as providing a highly social people with a chance to share one another's company. The political bonds between the Church and Irish Catholics became tighter still, with the Church providing the central organizing principles of everyday life, including the most intimate. The clergy kept a close watch over relations between men and women, and voices were raised to protest coeducational schools and unsupervised dancing. When the post-famine Irish Catholics left home for America, as they continued to do in great numbers, they brought with them their renewed devotion, their religious societies, and their parish-based sense of place and morals.

The Irish influence over the American Church's development was profound. Other Catholic immigrant groups brought their own traditions, but they were defenseless in the face of overwhelming numbers from Ireland on both sides of the altar. The German-American parish, for example, featured input from lay people unheard of in an Irish parish, and Italian-American pastors were less likely to emphasize weekly attendance at mass. The American Church as a whole, however, took on the stricter, more authoritarian

---

[2] **Vocations**—callings to a religious life; religious careers.

[3] **decimated**—destroyed or badly damaged.

character of the Irish parish as Ireland's exiles landed on the shores of New York, Boston, Philadelphia, and elsewhere. The Catholic population of America increased by a million (from 660,000 to 1.6 million) between 1840 and 1850, and the bulk of these new American Catholics were the Famine Irish, who brought with them a distinct identity based on their religion, an **abiding**[4] affection for the clergy who shared their sufferings, and a faith they had held on to even in the face of severe discrimination and bigotry. From that moment, everything about the American Church, from its insistence on a separate Catholic identity to the regulation of parishioners' sexual morals to the emphasis on clerical **hierarchy**,[5] **smacked**[6] of inherent Irishness. And it was no wonder. Thirteen of America's first seventeen cardinals boasted Irish roots, and the Irish dominated the Church rank and file of parish priests, to the occasional **chagrin**[7] of German, French, and Italian Catholics who sometimes requested, or demanded, their own national parishes with their own priests, thus accomplishing a segregation within the already segregated Catholic community. (For example, the small number of Lithuanians and Poles in Irish South Boston had their own parishes.)

Irish domination was as true of the **convent**[8] as it was of the **rectory**.[9] Historian Suellen Hoy of the University of Notre Dame notes that several thousand nuns left Ireland for America in two distinct waves during the nineteenth century. A Dublin educator named Sister Mary Eustace Eaton, who ran a school for girls from the city's working classes, single-handedly sent

---

[4] **abiding**—deep and lasting.

[5] **hierarchy**—group of persons of authority organized according to rank.

[6] **smacked**—had the distinctive flavor.

[7] **chagrin**—feeling of embarrassment or humiliation caused by failure or disappointment.

[8] **convent**—community of nuns; also, the building in which they live.

[9] **rectory**—the parish-owned house in which priests live.

four hundred Irish nuns to America in the late nineteenth century. They and many others crossed the Atlantic in response to pleas from Irish-American bishops who found themselves with hospitals to staff, schools to run, and social problems to address. Many of these women were among the most enthusiastic of immigrants, for Irish society offered them little save poverty and grinding routine.

Whether at the altar, in the schools, or in the pews, the Irish presence in the American Catholic Church was **ubiquitous**.[10] Orders of nuns from Ireland sent young women as far afield as gold-rush era California. The Christian Brothers of Ireland established Manhattan College in New York, La Salle University in Philadelphia, and Saint Mary's in California,[11] in addition to producing textbooks for use in American Catholic schools. The Irish came to dominate about half of Chicago's parishes by the turn of the century, despite widespread immigration to the Windy City by Catholic Poles and Lithuanians. In fact, Irish priests were everywhere Catholics were to be found in America. So **omnipresent**[12] was the Irish priest that he gained for himself a place in American popular culture, a distinction that brought with it decidedly mixed blessings.

In nineteenth-century America, there was no separating the Irish Catholic immigrants from their clergy. **Nativists**[13] invariably described Irish Catholic culture as "priest-ridden," a subculture susceptible to antidemocratic and anti-American plots hatched in the Vatican and executed by bishops and pastors. Samuel

---

[10] **ubiquitous**—everywhere.

[11] Golway is mistaken. The Christian Brothers of Ireland have only one institution of higher learning in the United States—Iona in New Rochelle, New York. The French Christian (De La Salle) Brothers established these schools.

[12] **omnipresent**—present everywhere at once.

[13] **Nativists**—those who favored the established population over immigrants.

Morse, inventor of the telegraph and one of the country's leading nativists, complained that Catholic immigrants obeyed "their priests as **demigods**."[14] The cartoonist Thomas Nast offered a graphic illustration of nativist fears in a cartoon that showed a wave of bishop-alligators landing on American shores to ravage decent Americans. Priests were seen, not entirely without evidence, as the shadow leaders of immigrant Catholics, and, as both priest and immigrant Catholic were perceived to be Irish, the anti-Catholicism that already was a feature of American life in the mid-nineteenth century easily translated into anti-Irish bias.

But by 1944, when [actor] Bing Crosby donned a Roman collar[15] and a Saint Louis Browns' cap for his role as the breezy Irish-American priest Father O'Malley in [the movie] *Going My Way*, America had made a peace of sorts with priest, parish, and parishioner. Irish Catholics were running most of the nation's important cities, and one, Al Smith, had even been nominated for President, with no apparent diminution of American liberties. The film **ratified**[16] the position of the Irish relative to the American Church, that is, the two were indistinguishable, at least in the public imagination. In *Going My Way*, all three priest characters are Irish, with a real-life Irish immigrant, [actor] Barry Fitzgerald, playing second fiddle to Crosby in the role of the aging pastor, Father Fitzgibbon. Fitzgerald's stage Irish accent was made for Hollywood, but his acting skills were more impressive. He was, after all, an Irish Protestant, as a generation of Irish Catholics pointed out with some amazement, and perhaps even a bit of horror.

---

[14] **demigods**—offspring of gods and mortals.

[15] **Roman collar**—the clerical collar worn by Catholic priests.

[16] **ratified**—formally approved, confirmed.

While *Going My Way* is hard to beat for pure *schmaltz*,[17] or should we say blarney, it remains the definitively romantic view of the Irish Catholic parish in the middle of twentieth-century America, when the second and third generations were dominant, and immigrants were those with gray hair and stooped posture. Saint Dominic's (Father O'Malley's parish) was intensely urban, filled with social problems (youth gangs, a hint of prostitution) that required priestly intervention, and populated with people who made it their business to know one another's business. Father Fitzgibbon knew that the local Irish cop hadn't been to church in ten years, and the neighborhood busybody, Mrs. Quimp (probably a widow, for her husband never is seen, and such parishes were populated with women whose men died young and exhausted) saw to it that the priests were kept informed of social, cultural, and political developments taking place on the streets and in the tenement flats. Saint Dominic's was the center of its parishioners' lives, and a trip outside its boundaries (to see a ball game) is about all the excitement for which anybody could ask. Why, *Going My Way* had it all, from **sainted**[18] mothers to an abiding reverence for the beverage referred to in Gaelic as *usquebagh* or, as English speakers say, whiskey.

Saint Dominic's, of course, was a Hollywood **confection**,[19] but as a glimpse of a world unknown to the majority of pre–World War II Americans, it served a useful purpose. At the time of *Going My Way*, Catholics still were outside mainstream American culture, their customs and rituals a mystery to most Americans. Filled with sentiment and all-around

---

[17] *schmaltz*—Yiddish for chicken fat; excessive sentimentality.

[18] **sainted**—respected as a saint.

[19] **confection**—piece displaying splendid craftsmanship, skill, and work, like an elaborate sugar decoration.

Americanism, even with the occasional ethnic reference thrown in, the film portrayed the Irish Catholic parish as benevolent, utterly nonthreatening, and, in the end, an important socializing force in American urban life. That was a far cry from the popular image of priests, parish, and parishioners that a young Father Fitzgibbon might have confronted at the beginning of his fictional career.

QUESTIONS TO CONSIDER

1. How did post-Famine-era Irish Catholics in America differ from those who came before?

2. Why did German, French, and Italian Catholics demand their own national parishes and priests?

3. Why would anti-Irish persecution by nativists make Irish Catholics more likely to seek refuge in parish life? Why would nativists see this behavior as threatening?

4. What role did the movie Going My Way have in diminishing anti-Catholic prejudice in the United States and how did it mirror Irish Catholic parish life?

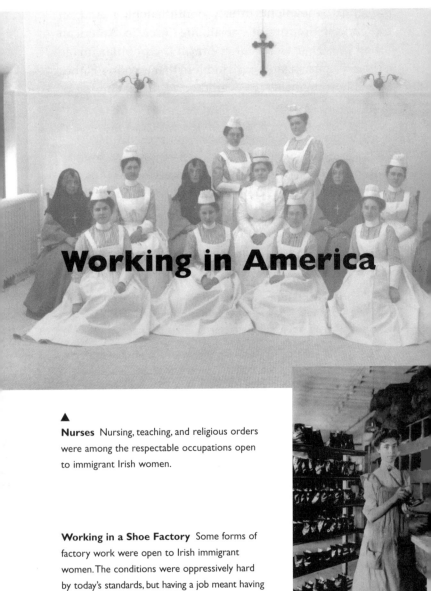

Working in America

▲
Nurses Nursing, teaching, and religious orders were among the respectable occupations open to immigrant Irish women.

Working in a Shoe Factory Some forms of factory work were open to Irish immigrant women. The conditions were oppressively hard by today's standards, but having a job meant having an income—money to send home, to support oneself, even to provide a little enjoyment. ▶

▲

Servant Many immigrants obtained work in various serving occupations, as domestic workers, maids, babies' nurses, or cooks, for example.

▲

Progress? These trading cards betray the racial bigotry aimed at early immigrants as they show an unappealing Irishman's movement up the social ladder from immigrant to laborer to policeman and politician.

Irish Cop The police forces of northern cities provided jobs for immigrant men, and the Irish cop became a fixture, bringing security to city streets and amusement to comedians, writers, and cartoonists. ▶

▲

Molly Maguires In 1877, fifty Irish coal miners in Pennsylvania were charged with conspiracy to commit murder. The prosecutors were employed by the mining and railroad companies, and the defendants were all members of the Ancient Order of Hibernians. Forty were convicted, twenty were sent to prison, and twenty were hanged.

Mother Jones Mary Harris, born in Cork City, Ireland, was also known as the "Angel of the Mines," and "the most dangerous woman in America." A well-known labor leader from 1890–1930, she advised her followers to "pray for the dead and fight like hell for the living." ▶

The Baltimore & Ohio Railroad Strike In this confrontation, Irish-American miners were led by Terence V. Powderly, founder of the Knights of Labor, while mine owners had a strong ally in the Irish-American Governor of Maryland, John Lee Carroll. This print shows a Maryland National Guard Regiment firing on a crowd of strikers and their families.
▼

▲

Elizabeth Gurley Flynn This labor organizer, agitator, and socialist was a founder of the American Civil Liberties Union. She joined the Industrial Workers of the World in 1907, and fought for workers' rights in New York, Massachusetts, New Jersey, Washington, and Montana.

▲

Child Labor Often immigrant children were called upon to help support their families. This print shows "Mrs. Donovan and her 6 children, ages 4 to 13, tying tags for Dennison Co. on the steps of their Roxbury, Mass., home."

Opportunities and Responsibilities

from

Teacher

BY HELEN KELLER

*When Helen Keller entered Radcliffe College in 1900, she was
already world-famous. She had been deaf, blind, and unable to speak
since the age of 19 months. Thanks to her heroic Irish-American
teacher, Annie Sullivan, young Helen became an independent learner
and a writer. Her journey from darkness to light fascinated millions
and her autobiography,* The Story of My Life, *caused a sensation.
William Gibson dramatized Sullivan's struggle to teach Keller in a
play, "The Miracle Worker," and in 1962 the play was made into
a successful film. Keller graduated cum laude from Radcliffe, learned
French without braille, and became a lecturer and advocate for the
blind. Annie Sullivan became famous herself because of Keller's
writing. In 1926, shortly before her death, she accepted an honorary
degree from Temple University.*

A daughter of Irish immigrants, at that time the most
despised social group in the Northeast, Annie Sullivan
was born in squalid poverty on April 4, 1866, in Feeding
Hills, Massachusetts, and as far back as she could
remember she had had trouble with her eyes. They still

bothered her. Her mother died when she was eight years old, leaving two other children. Her father abandoned all three two years later and Annie never learned what became of him. Her younger sister Mary was placed with relatives and Annie and her seven-year-old brother Jimmie were sent to the State Infirmary, the **almshouse**,[1] at Tewksbury, Annie because she was difficult to manage and too blind to be useful, Jimmie because he was becoming helplessly lame with a tubercular hip.

They entered the almshouse in February 1876 and Jimmie died in May. Annie stayed four years. No one outside was interested in her and she had no friends but her fellow paupers. It was one of them who told her that there were special schools for the blind and as time went on—she lost track of time in Tewksbury—her desire for an education grew. To escape from the pit of **degradation**[2] and disease in which she lived seemed impossible until the stench from the almshouse rose so high that the State Board of Charities ordered an investigation. The investigators did not discover her. The inmates knew the name of the chairman and when the committee members arrived she flung herself towards them, unable to distinguish one from another, and cried out, "Mr. Sanborn, Mr. Sanborn, I want to go to school!"

She reached the Perkins Institution in October 1880 and there, at the age of fourteen, began her education by learning to read with her fingers. The school had no facilities for taking care of its pupils during vacations and when summer came she was put out to work in a rooming house in Boston. Through one of the lodgers she found her way to the Massachusetts Eye and Ear Infirmary and in August Dr. Bradford performed an operation on her left eye. The next August he attended to the right eye and when the operations were over Annie could see well enough to read in the ordinary way

---

[1] **almshouse**—housing for the poor who could not work, funded by charity.

[2] **degradation**—state of reduced worth, quality, or standing.

for limited periods of time, but not well enough to warrant transfer to a school for the seeing. She remained at Perkins for six years, graduating in 1886 as **valedictorian**[3] of her class. The school had done what it could. The rest was up to her.

She recognized her handicaps—her meager years of education, her lack of contact with the **amenities**[4] of gracious living, and, above all, her uncertain, **precarious**[5] sight—but she had hoped for something more exciting than looking after a deaf-blind child. Captain Keller's[6] offer was the best she had. After she had accepted it she spent some months reading Dr. Howe's reports[7] on Laura Bridgman, a painful task because of her eyes. She already knew the manual alphabet. Like her schoolmates, she had learned it so as to talk with Laura, who was still **cloistered**[8] at the Perkins Institution because she had never been able to adapt herself to any other kind of life. And yet Laura was the mark to aim at. No other deaf-blind person had come near the peak upon which she stood.

Red-eyed from another operation on her eyes and from crying with homesickness, Annie Sullivan arrived in Tuscumbia on March 3, 1887, a date that Helen has always cherished as her "soul's birthday." She began at once spelling into Helen's hand, suiting the word to the action, the action to the word, and the child responded by imitating the finger motions like a bright, inquisitive animal. It took a month to reach the human mind. On April 5, a date not second to March 3 in importance, the Phantom Helen made contact with reality. While Annie Sullivan pumped water over her hand it came to the

---

[3] **valedictorian**—student with the highest scholastic achievement in his or her graduating class.

[4] **amenities**—things that increase material comfort or enjoyment.

[5] **precarious**—uncertain, endangered.

[6] Captain Keller's—belonging to Helen Keller's father.

[7] Dr. Lucien Howe (1848–1928) was a distinguished ophthamologist responsible for the law requiring newborn babies to have eye drops to prevent blindness.

[8] **cloistered**—secluded, as in a convent or monastery.

child in a flash that water, wherever it was found, was water, and that the finger motions she had just felt on her palm meant water and nothing else. In that thrilling moment she found the key to her kingdom. Everything had a name and she had a way to learn the names. She formed a question by pointing to Annie Sullivan. "Teacher," Annie replied.

From that date Helen's progress was so rapid that educators soon became aware that a great teacher was at work, greater even than Dr. Howe. At the age of ten Helen announced that she was going to learn to talk with her mouth like other people instead of with her fingers like a deaf person, and when, after eleven lessons in oral speech she was able to say, however haltingly, "I-am-not-dumb-now," there seemed no limit to what she might achieve. . . .

Naturally little Helen was aware of Teacher only as a loving guiding person with an enchanting gift of imparting knowledge. Annie never cast the shadow of her years in the almshouse at Tewksbury upon the joyous mind of a child growing up in normal surroundings. She kept that dark secret until she was sixty-four and I was fifty. But she talked freely to me as a child about the village of Feeding Hills, Massachusetts, where she was born, and about her little brother Jimmie over whose death she had grieved so passionately. My eager questions about her family led her on to spell[9] stories about her sister Mary and other girls she had known and tales of the little people of Ireland[10] that her father had told her. Thus another **exquisite**[11] bond of sympathy was woven between the lonely woman and her pupil.

Annie did not allow any complaint of her loneliness to escape from her, but as I look back upon those early years, I am struck by the confidence with which she

---

[9] spell—use her hands to spell out in sign language.

[10] little people of Ireland—leprechauns and other fairies from Irish myths.

[11] **exquisite**—of such beauty and delicacy as to arouse delight.

moved among the fires of creation that bring normal personalities out of unpromising materials. She was exploring an area which aroused in her all the instincts of selfless desire, adventure, and aspiration to great accomplishment. There had been no one else on record who regarded a deaf-blind creature (I use the word literally, a *creature* of circumstances) as capable of attaining normality to more than a small degree, and behold, there was Annie Sullivan soaring on the fiery wings of that dream! How she conceived it and why she persevered all her life towards the goal she called "perfection" I do not know, but from bits of talk I caught on her fingers, I know that in her mind there were lovely visions, now radiant, now dimmed through disappointment, of "an angel child," "a maiden fair and full of grace," "a young woman pleading the cause of the unfortunate with a natural voice," and other images whose nonrealization makes tears start to my eyes. As I have often touched fruit blossoms fluttering lacelike on a tree, so the exquisiteness of Annie's generous ambitions for my self-fulfillment comes back to charm and awe me. Imaginatively she peeped into every cradle, expecting to discover a splendid new version of humanity.

QUESTIONS TO CONSIDER

1. How might Annie's struggle to escape the almshouse at Tewksbury have prepared her to teach Helen?

2. Helen refers to herself as the "Phantom Helen" before she responded to Annie's teaching. Why might she name herself that way?

3. Why did Annie wait so long to tell her pupil about her horrible experiences at Tewksbury?

4. What opportunities were open to Annie? How did she take advantage of them?

Honest Graft and Dishonest Graft

BY GEORGE WASHINGTON PLUNKITT

Tammany Hall began in 1789 as a New York City social society, but quickly developed into a powerful political "machine" for the newly created Democratic Party. The Tammany "spoils system"— which rewarded loyal supporters of successful candidates with government jobs—helped win the presidency for Andrew Jackson in 1828. Tammany originally had been anti-immigrant, but the influx of Famine-era Irish to New York City changed that. The Irish were a powerful voting bloc that wanted the jobs, housing, social services, and rewards Tammany could deliver. William "Boss" Tweed took charge of Tammany in 1862 and used it to enrich himself and friends with millions of tax dollars until evidence of the fraud surfaced. "Honest John" Kelly, an Irish Catholic, replaced Tweed and created a structure organized from the block captain to the precinct captain to the ward boss. George Washington Plunkitt was a key Tammany player in the early years of the twentieth century. He explained his "political" views in William Riordan's classic work, Plunkitt of Tammany Hall.

Everybody is talkin' these days about Tammany men growin' rich on **graft**,[1] but nobody thinks of drawin' the distinction between honest graft and dishonest graft. There's all the difference in the world between the two. Yes, many of our men have grown rich in politics. I have myself. I've made a big fortune out of the game, and I'm gettin' richer every day, but I've not gone in for dishonest graft—blackmailin' gamblers, saloonkeepers, disorderly people, etc.—and neither has any of the men who have made big fortunes in politics.

There's an honest graft, and I'm an example of how it works. I might sum up the whole thing by sayin': "I seen my opportunities and I took 'em."

Just let me explain by examples. My [Democratic] party's in power in the city, and it's goin' to undertake a lot of public improvements. Well, I'm tipped off, say, that they're going to lay out a new park at a certain place.

I see my opportunity and I take it. I go to that place and I buy up all the land I can in the neighborhood. Then the board of this or that makes its plan public, and there is a rush to get my land, which nobody cared particular for before.

Ain't it perfectly honest to charge a good price and make a profit on my investment and foresight? Of course, it is. Well, that's honest graft.

Or supposin' it's a new bridge they're goin' to build. I get tipped off and I buy as much property as I can that has to be taken for approaches. I sell at my own price later on and drop some more money in the bank.

Wouldn't you? It's just like lookin' ahead in Wall Street or in the coffee or cotton market. It's honest graft, and I'm lookin' for it every day in the year. I will tell you frankly that I've got a good lot of it, too.

---

[1] **graft**—the unscrupulous use of one's position to derive profit or advantages.

I'll tell you of one case. They were goin' to fix up a big park, no matter where. I got on to it, and went lookin' about for land in that neighborhood.

I could get nothin' at a bargain but a big piece of swamp, but I took it fast enough and held on to it. What turned out was just what I counted on. They couldn't make the park complete without Plunkitt's swamp, and they had to pay a good price for it. Anything dishonest in that?

Up in the watershed I made some money, too. I bought up several bits of land there some years ago and made a pretty good guess that they would be bought up for water purposes later by the city.

Somehow, I always guessed about right, and shouldn't I enjoy the profit of my foresight? It was rather amusin' when the condemnation commissioners[2] came along and found piece after piece of the land in the name of George Plunkitt of the Fifteenth Assembly District, New York City. They wondered how I knew just what to buy. The answer is—I seen my opportunity and I took it. I haven't confined myself to land; anything that pays is in my line.

For instance, the city is repavin' a street and has several hundred thousand old granite blocks to sell. I am on hand to buy, and I know just what they are worth.

How? Never mind that. I had a sort of monopoly of this business for a while, but once a newspaper tried to do me. It got some outside men to come over from Brooklyn and New Jersey to bid against me.

Was I done? Not much. I went to each of the men and said: "How many of these two hundred and fifty thousand stones do you want?" One said twenty thousand, and another wanted fifteen thousand, and another wanted ten thousand. I said: "All right, let me bid for the lot, and I'll give each of you all you want for nothin'."

[2] condemnation commissioners—government officials who acquired land for public use.

They agreed, of course. Then the auctioneer yelled: "How much am I bid for these two hundred and fifty thousand fine pavin' stones?"

"Two dollars and fifty cents," says I.

"Two dollars and fifty cents!" screamed the auctioneer. "Oh, that's a joke! Give me a real bid."

He found the bid was real enough. My rivals stood silent. I got the lot for $2.50 and gave them their share. That's how the attempt to do Plunkitt ended, and that's how all such attempts end.

I've told you how I got rich by honest graft. Now, let me tell you that most politicians who are accused of robbin' the city get rich the same way.

They didn't steal a dollar from the city treasury. They just seen their opportunities and took them. That is why, when a reform administration comes in and spends a half million dollars in tryin' to find the public robberies they talked about in the campaign, they don't find them.

The books are always all right. The money in the city treasury is all right. Everything is all right. All they can show is that the Tammany heads of departments looked after their friends, within the law, and gave them what opportunities they could to make honest graft. Now, let me tell you that's never goin' to hurt Tammany with the people. Every good man looks after his friends, and any man who doesn't isn't likely to be popular. If I have a good thing to hand out in private life, I give it to a friend. Why shouldn't I do the same in public life?

Another kind of honest graft. Tammany has raised a good many salaries. There was an awful howl by the reformers, but don't you know that Tammany gains ten votes for every one it lost by salary raisin'?

The Wall Street banker thinks it shameful to raise a department clerk's salary from $1,500 to $1,800 a year, but every man who draws a salary himself says: "That's all right. I wish it was me." And he feels very much like votin' the Tammany ticket on election day, just out of sympathy.

Tammany was beat in 1901 because the people were deceived into believin' that it worked dishonest graft. They didn't draw a distinction between dishonest and honest graft, but they saw that some Tammany men grew rich, and supposed they had been robbin' the city treasury or levyin' blackmail on disorderly houses, or workin' in with the gamblers and lawbreakers.

As a matter of policy, if nothing else, why should the Tammany leaders go into such dirty business, when there is so much honest graft lyin' around when they are in power? Did you ever consider that?

Now, in conclusion, I want to say that I don't own a dishonest dollar. If my worst enemy was given the job of writin' my **epitaph**[3] when I'm gone, he couldn't do more than write:

"George W. Plunkitt. He Seen His Opportunities, and He Took 'Em."

---

[3] **epitaph**—words placed on a dead person's tombstone to sum up his or her life.

QUESTIONS TO CONSIDER

1. What opportunities are open to George Plunkitt? How does he take advantage of them?

2. How does Plunkitt explain that his kind of graft is "honest"?

3. What is wrong in what Plunkitt does? Who gets hurt?

4. What examples of similar activities are going on in government, business, or finance today?

from

To Hell and Back

BY AUDIE MURPHY

*Irish-American Audie Murphy was born in rural Texas in 1924.
His parents were poor sharecroppers, and Audie was the oldest
of nine children. When his father abandoned the family, Murphy
left school and took over the role of father. After the death of his
mother, he joined the U.S. Army, worked his way up to officer's
rank, and fought against the German army in Europe during World
War II. Murphy displayed such bravery that he was awarded the
Congressional Medal of Honor and became the war's most decorated
soldier. He tried to give the credit to his fellow soldiers who had
been killed in combat, and it was said that he took care of his men
the same way he took care of his younger brothers and sisters.
After the war, Murphy became a successful movie actor. He played
himself in the movie based on his autobiography,* To Hell and
Back, *and starred in a number of Westerns. He died in a plane
crash in 1971 and is buried in Arlington National Cemetery. This
excerpt from the book describes his battlefield actions.*

We reach the edge of the forest. For two hours the
night is filled with the clump, clump of pick and shovel
gnawing at the rock-hard earth. The efforts are futile, but

the exercise keeps us from freezing. When we finally give up trying to chew holes in the ground, we stamp up and down a narrow road winding through the woods to stir up heat in our bodies.

As the dirty, gray light of dawn spreads over the **terrain**,[1] a tension grips us. To the infantryman, daybreak is the critical hour. It is the customary time for attacking or being attacked. Our support has not yet arrived.

I contact battalion headquarters.

"Any change in orders for Company B?"

"No. Hold on to your position. Our attack is going to be delayed."

I hang up the receiver and study the landscape tactically. We are at the butt-end of a rough U, whose sides are formed by fingerlike extensions of the woods stretching toward Holtzwihr. Directly before us are flat open fields beyond which I can see a church steeple and housetops in the village, a mile away. The narrow road over which we have been pounding our feet leads from the woods to the town. A drainage ditch flanks its right side. Underbrush near the forest edge has been cleared away to furnish fire breaks for the enemy.

During the night, two tank destroyers have moved up to our position. They have parked on the road; and most of the crew members are asleep. Rousing the lieutenant in charge, I say,

"You'd better get your TDs[2] under cover. They're like ducks sitting in the road."

He climbs out through the **turret**,[3] yawning.

"If we get off, we'll get stuck."

"You've got no cover there."

"If the krauts[4] attack, we can see them coming."

---

[1] **terrain**—tract of land; ground.

[2] TDs—tank destroyers, battlefield vehicles.

[3] **turret**—a heavily armored enclosure containing mounted guns and their gunners.

[4] krauts—army slang for the enemy German soldiers, from the word *sauerkraut,* a traditional German food.

"Okay, it's your funeral."

Just across the road, the platoon machine-gun squad has set up its weapon under a tree.

"What's happened to the attack?" the squad sergeant asks.

"It's been held up."

He whistles and shakes his head. "How long do you think this beat-up outfit could stand off a counterattack?"

"I don't know. How's your ammunition?"

"We've got about four hundred rounds."

"Make it all count, if we are attacked."

"I don't aim to do any practicing."

Checking the other men, I find that our right flank is exposed. Some unit failed to get up on schedule.

The morning drags by. A forward artillery observer with a radio joins us. The icy tree branches rattle in the wind.

Again I contact headquarters.

"What about orders?"

"No change. Hold your position."

At two o'clock in the afternoon, I see the Germans lining up for an attack. Six tanks rumble to the outskirts of Holtzwihr, split into groups of threes, and fan out toward either side of the clearing. Obviously they intend an encircling movement, using the fingers of trees for cover. I yell to my men to get ready.

Then wave after wave of white dots, barely **discernible**[5] against the background of snow, start across the field. They are enemy infantrymen, wearing snowcapes and advancing in a staggered skirmish formation.

One of our tank destroyers starts its engine and maneuvers for a firing position. It slides into a ditch at an angle that leaves the turret guns completely useless. The driver steps on the gas; the tank wallows further into the ditch; the engine dies. The crew bails out and takes off for the rear.

---

[5] **discernible**—visible.

"I'm trying to contact headquarters," shouts the artillery observer.

I had forgotten about him. We cannot afford to have the radio captured.

"Get to the rear," I holler. "I'll get the artillery by phone."

"I don't want to leave you."

"Get going. You can't do any good. Just take care of that radio."

I grab a map, estimate the enemy's position, and seize the field telephone.

"Battalion," cheerfully answers a headquarters lieutenant.

"This is Murphy. We're being attacked. Get me the artillery."

"Coming up."

I want a round of smoke at co-ordinates 30.5–60; and tell those joes to shake the lead out."

"How many krauts?"

"Six tanks that I can see, and maybe a couple hundred foot soldiers supporting."

"Good God! How close?"

"Close enough. Give me that artillery."

I hang up the receiver and grab my **carbine**[6] just as the enemy's preliminary barrage hits. It is murderous. A single tree burst knocks out our machine-gun squad. The second tank destroyer is hit flush, and three of its crew are killed. The remainder, coughing and half-blinded, climb from the smoking turret and sprint down the road to the rear. At that moment I know that we are lost.

The smoke shell whizzes over, landing beyond the oncoming Germans.

Two hundred [yards] right; two hundred over.[7] And fire for effect.

---

[6] **carbine**—rifle.

[7] Murphy means that his artillery fire has hit two hundred yards right of and two hundred yards over the heads of the advancing enemy infantrymen.

Our counterbarrage is on the nose. A line of enemy infantrymen disappear in a cloud of smoke and snow. But others keep coming.

The telephone rings.

"How close are they?"

"Fifty over, and keep firing for effect."[8] That artillery curtain must be kept between us and the enemy.

The tanks are now close enough to rake our position with machine-gun fire. Of the hundred and twenty-eight men that began the drive, not over forty remain. And I am the last of seven officers. Trying to stop the armor with our small arms is useless. I yell to the men to start pulling out.

"What about you?" shouts Kohl.

"I'm staying up with the phone as long as I can. Get the men back, and keep them grouped. Candler will help you."

"Candler's dead,"

The telephone rings.

"How close are they?"

"Fifty over, and keep blasting. The company's pulling back."

I raise my eyes and see that the men are hesitating. Clapping down the receiver, I yell, "Get the hell out of here. That's an order!"

Kohl says something, but his words are lost in a shell burst. He shrugs his shoulders, beckons with his thumb, and the men stumble through the woods, casting worried glances backward.

I seize my carbine and start sniping. The advance wave of infantrymen is within two hundred yards of my position.

The telephone rings.

"How close are they?"

"Fifty over. Keep it coming."

Dropping the receiver, I grab the carbine and fire until I give out of ammunition. As I turn to run, I notice

---

[8] He is asking the artillery to aim fifty yards closer and to keep on firing.

the burning tank destroyer. On its turret is a perfectly good machine gun and several cases of ammunition. The German tanks have suddenly veered to the left.

I change my plans and drag the telephone to the top of the tank destroyer. The body of the lieutenant with whom I talked early in the morning is sprawled over the edge of the hatch. His throat has been cut; a small river of blood streams down the side of the tank destroyer. I finish dragging the body out and dump it into the snow.

The telephone rings.

"How close are they?"

"Fifty over, and keep firing for effect."

"How close are they to your position?"

"Just hold the phone and I'll let you talk to one of the [expletive]."

Hastily checking the machine gun, I find that it has not been damaged. When I press the trigger, the chatter of the gun is like sweet music. Three krauts stagger and crumple in the snow.

Crash! The tank destroyer shudders violently. Vaguely I put two and two together and conclude that the TD has received another direct hit.

The telephone rings.

"This is Sergeant Bowes. Are you still alive, lieutenant?"

"Momentarily." I spread the map on my left palm. "Correct fire: —"[9]

Crash! I am conscious of a flash and explosion. I reel back with the map and telephone receiver in my hands.

"Lieutenant. Lieutenant. Can you hear me? Are you still alive, lieutenant?"

"I think so. Correct fire: Fifty over, and keep the line open."

I feed another belt of cartridges into the machine gun and seize the trigger again. The smoke is so thick that I can barely see through it; and the smell of smoldering

---

[9] Murphy is telling the sergeant to correct the aim of his men's gunfire.

flesh is again in my nostrils. But when the wind blows the smoke aside, I bore into any object that stirs.

The gun has thrown the krauts into confusion. Evidently they cannot locate its position. Later I am told that the burning tank destroyer, loaded with gasoline and ammunition, was expected to blow up any minute. That was why the enemy tanks gave it a wide berth and the infantrymen could not conceive of a man's using it for cover.

I do not know about that. For the time being my imagination is gone; and my numbed brain is intent only on destroying. I am conscious only that the smoke and the turret afford a good screen, and that, for the first time in three days, my feet are warm.

Now the Germans try a new tactic. A gust of wind whips the smoke aside; and I see an enemy sergeant in the roadside ditch not thirty yards from my position. He peers cautiously about, then turns his head and motions his squad forward. As I spin my gun barrel upon him, a billow of smoke comes between us.

For a minute or so I wait. The tree branches overhead stir stiffly in the gust, the smoke column folds to one side. The twelve Germans, huddled like partridges in the ditch, are discussing something, perhaps my possible location. I press the trigger and slowly traverse the barrel. The twelve bodies slump in a stack position. I give them another methodically thorough burst, and pick up the phone.

"Correct fire, battalion. Fifty over."

"Are you all right, lieutenant?"

"I'm all right, sergeant. What are *your* postwar plans?"

The barrage lands within fifty yards of the tank destroyer. The shouting, screaming Germans caught in it are silent now. The enemy tanks, reluctant to advance further without infantry support, lumber back toward Holtzwihr.

I snatch the telephone receiver. "Sergeant. Sergeant Bowes. Correct fire: Fifty over; and keep firing for effect. This is my last change."

"Fifty over? That's your own position."[10]

"I don't give a [expletive]. Fifty over."

Concussion from the enemy barrage almost knocks me from the tank destroyer. For a moment I am stunned; and then I see the telephone receiver in my hand.

"Sergeant Bowes. Battalion. Sergeant." There is no answer. The telephone line has been knocked out.

My cloudy brain slowly directs my actions. Carefully I fold the field map and notice that it has been riddled with shell fragments. I examine my hands and arms. They are unscratched.

A dull pain throbs in my right leg. Looking down, I see that the trouser leg is bloody. That does not matter.

As if under the influence of some drug, I slide off the tank destroyer and, without once looking back, walk down the road through the forest. If the Germans want to shoot me, let them. I am too weak from fear and exhaustion to care.

---

[10] Sergeant Bows means that if they aim yet another fifty yards closer to Murphy they will hit him.

QUESTIONS TO CONSIDER

1. How does Murphy try to prepare his men for possible German attack?

2. Why does Murphy tell his men to retreat? Do they want to leave him behind?

3. How does Murphy portray himself and his bravery under strong enemy fire?

John Kennedy's Inaugural Address

BY PRESIDENT JOHN F. KENNEDY

The thirty-fifth President of the United States, John Fitzgerald Kennedy, was born in 1917 in Brookline, Massachusetts, to a wealthy family directly descended from Irish Famine emigrants. Young John, or "Jack" as he was called, attended Choate prep school, Princeton, and then Harvard. During World War II, Kennedy became a hero when he led the rescue of his men after his boat, the PT 109, was rammed and sunk by a Japanese ship. When he returned to the United States, his father created a campaign machine that put Kennedy in Congress. In 1952, he won a seat in the U.S. Senate, and then received a Pulitzer Prize for his book, Profiles in Courage. Kennedy's good looks, articulate speech, sense of humor, Harvard education, and Massachusetts accent all helped make him "charismatic," and the perfect presidential candidate for the dawning television age. In 1960, Kennedy became the youngest President ever elected, the first President born in the twentieth century, and the first Catholic president ever. He served exactly 1,000 days in office before being assassinated on November 22, 1963.

Vice President Johnson, Mr. Speaker, Mr. Chief Justice, President Eisenhower, Vice President Nixon, President Truman, Reverend Clergy, fellow citizens:

We observe today not a victory of party but a celebration of freedom—symbolizing an end as well as a beginning—signifying renewal as well as change. For I have sworn before you and Almighty God the same solemn oath our **forebears**[1] prescribed nearly a century and three quarters ago.

The world is very different now. For man holds in his mortal hands the power to abolish all forms of human poverty and all forms of human life. And yet the same revolutionary beliefs for which our forebears fought are still at issue around the globe—the belief that the rights of man come not from the generosity of the state but from the hand of God.

We dare not forget today that we are the heirs of that first revolution. Let the word go forth from this time and place, to friend and foe alike, that the torch has been passed to a new generation of Americans—born in this century, tempered by war, disciplined by a hard and bitter peace, proud of our ancient heritage—and unwilling to witness or permit the slow undoing of those human rights to which this nation has always been committed, and to which we are committed today at home and around the world.

Let every nation know, whether it wishes us well or ill, that we shall pay any price, bear any burden, meet any hardship, support any friend, oppose any foe to assure the survival and the success of liberty.

This much we pledge—and more.

To those old allies whose cultural and spiritual origins we share, we pledge the loyalty of faithful friends. United, there is little we cannot do in a host of cooperative ventures. Divided, there is little we can do—for we dare not meet a powerful challenge at odds and split **asunder**.[2]

---

[1] **forebears**—ancestors.

[2] **asunder**—in separate parts or pieces.

To those new states whom we welcome to the ranks of the free, we pledge our word that one form of colonial control shall not have passed away merely to be replaced by a far more iron tyranny. We shall not always expect to find them supporting our view. But, we shall always hope to find them strongly supporting their own freedom—and to remember that, in the past, those who foolishly sought power by riding the back of the tiger ended up inside.

To those peoples in the huts and villages of half the globe struggling to break the bonds of mass misery, we pledge our best efforts to help them help themselves, for whatever period is required—not because the Communists may be doing it, not because we seek their votes, but because it is right. If a free society cannot help the many who are poor, it cannot save the few who are rich.

To our sister republics south of our border, we offer a special pledge—to convert our good words into good deeds—in a new alliance for progress—to assist free men and free governments in casting off the chains of poverty. But this peaceful revolution of hope cannot become the prey of hostile powers. Let all our neighbors know that we shall join with them to oppose aggression or subversion anywhere in the Americas. And let every other power know that this Hemisphere intends to remain the master of its own house.

To that world assembly of sovereign states, the United Nations, our last best hope in an age where the instruments of war have far outpaced the instruments of peace, we renew our pledge of support—to prevent it from becoming merely a forum for **invective**[3]—to strengthen its shield of the new and the weak—and to enlarge the area in which its **writ**[4] may run.

Finally, to those nations who would make themselves our adversary, we offer not a pledge but a request: that both sides begin anew the quest for peace, before the

---

[3] **invective**—abusive language.

[4] **writ**—jurisdiction, authority.

dark powers of destruction unleashed by science engulf all humanity in planned or accidental self-destruction.

We dare not tempt them with weakness. For only when our arms are sufficient beyond doubt can we be certain beyond doubt that they will never be employed.

But neither can two great and powerful groups of nations take comfort from our present course—both sides overburdened by the cost of modern weapons, both rightly alarmed by the steady spread of the deadly atom, yet both racing to alter that uncertain balance of terror that stays the hand of mankind's final war.

So let us begin anew—remembering on both sides that civility is not a sign of weakness, and sincerity is always subject to proof. Let us never negotiate out of fear. But let us never fear to negotiate.

Let both sides explore what problems unite us instead of **belaboring**[5] those problems which divide us.

Let both sides, for the first time, formulate serious and precise proposals for the inspection and control of arms—and bring the absolute power to destroy other nations under the absolute control of all nations.

Let both sides seek to invoke the wonders of science instead of its terrors. Together let us explore the stars, conquer the deserts, **eradicate**[6] disease, tap the ocean depths, and encourage the arts and commerce.

Let both sides unite to heed in all corners of the earth the command of Isaiah—to "undo the heavy burdens . . . (and) let the oppressed go free."

And if a beach-head of cooperation may push back the jungle of suspicion, let both sides join in creating a new **endeavor**,[7] not a new balance of power, but a new world of law, where the strong are just and the weak secure and the peace preserved.

---

[5] **belaboring**—attacking verbally.

[6] **eradicate**—get rid of.

[7] **endeavor**—conscientious or concerted effort.

All this will not be finished in the first one hundred days. Nor will it be finished in the first one thousand days, nor in the life of this Administration, nor even perhaps in our lifetime on this planet. But let us begin.

In your hands, my fellow citizens, more than mine, will rest the final success or failure of our course. Since this country was founded, each generation of Americans has been summoned to give testimony to its national loyalty. The graves of young Americans who answered the call to service surround the globe.

Now the trumpet summons us again not as a call to bear arms, though arms we need—not as a call to battle, though embattled we are—but a call to bear the burden of a long twilight struggle, year in and year out, "rejoicing in hope, patient in tribulation"—a struggle against the common enemies of man: tyranny, poverty, disease and war itself.

Can we forge against these enemies a grand and global alliance, North and South, East and West, that can assure a more fruitful life for all mankind? Will you join in that historic effort?

In the long history of the world, only a few generations have been granted the role of defending freedom in its hour of maximum danger. I do not shrink from this responsibility—I welcome it. I do not believe that any of us would exchange places with any other people or any other generation. The energy, the faith, the devotion which we bring to this endeavor will light our country and all who serve it—and the glow from that fire can truly light the world.

And so, my fellow Americans: ask not what your country can do for you—ask what you can do for your country.

My fellow citizens of the world: ask not what America will do for you, but what together we can do for the freedom of man.

Finally, whether you are citizens of America or citizens of the world, ask of us here the same high standards of strength and sacrifice which we ask of you. With a good conscience our only sure reward, with history the final judge of our deeds, let us go forth to lead the land we love, asking His blessing and His help, but knowing that here on earth God's work must truly be our own.

QUESTIONS TO CONSIDER

1. Kennedy asserts that our rights do not come from the "generosity of the state." From where does he say they come? Do you agree?

2. Kennedy says the trumpet summons us to struggle against "the common enemies of man." What are they?

3. Kennedy mentions the "balance of terror." To what does he refer?

4. What is Kennedy saying about the opportunities and responsibilities of citizenship?

The Leader Who Led

BY THEODORE C. SORENSON

The Cuban Missile Crisis in 1962 took place at the height of Cold War competition between the Soviet Union and the United States. The U.S. had a major advantage since Soviet missiles were only powerful enough to be launched against U.S. allies in Europe, while American missiles in Turkey could strike the entire Soviet Union. Cuba, under the leadership of Fidel Castro, was the only Communist country and only Soviet ally in the Western Hemisphere. Nikita Khrushchev, the Soviet premier, decided to place missiles in Cuba that could deliver nuclear warheads to U.S. cities. After a spy plane photographed the construction of these missile sites, President John Kennedy revealed their presence and declared that any nuclear missile launched from Cuba would be regarded as an attack on the U.S. by the Soviet Union. The ensuing crisis—described here by a key Kennedy aide in a 1997 newspaper article—brought the world to the very brink of nuclear war.

While reading the newly published transcripts of the deliberations of President John F. Kennedy and his advisers during the Cuban missile crisis of 1962, I recalled the chilling question from the floor of a religious **convocation**[1] that I addressed some months after the crisis ended: "By what authority, Mr. Sorensen, did President Kennedy last October threaten the **incineration**[2] of 190 million Americans?"

It was a fair question, with no wholly satisfactory answer then or now. As these transcripts remind us, the possibility of setting a fatal match to the global nuclear tinderbox in which we all lived during the Cold War did indeed hang over the President and his advisers throughout the 13 days and nights we met in October 1962. No person or persons had the authority to knowingly light that particular match. No person ever should.

President Kennedy did take our case to the United Nations—but not to ask for intervention or authorization. He sought instead to use that unique world forum to put the Soviets on the defensive diplomatically for their sudden and **surreptitious**[3] installation of strategic nuclear missiles 90 miles from our shores.

In this, Kennedy succeeded. The quiet communications to both sides by U Thant, the Secretary General of the United Nations, and the world's condemnation of Nikita Khrushchev's action were of help in the crucial days that followed.

More important from a legal point of view, Kennedy asked our neighbors in the Organization of American States to both authorize and participate in our naval blockade of Cuba (termed a "Quarantine Against Offensive Weapons" to make it sound less **belligerent**[4]). That elevated the blockade to an act of regional self-defense under international law. But even before approaching the O.A.S., Kennedy had decided that he

---

[1] **convocation**—assembly.

[2] **incineration**—destruction by fire.

[3] **surreptitious**—secret, clandestine, or stealthy.

[4] **belligerent**—hostile or aggressive.

had no choice but to proceed, with or without any endorsements from the international community.

But what was he to do at home, consistent with "government by the consent of the governed"? He was not willing to be guided by a quick public opinion poll, much less the mass of demonstrators and counter-demonstrators who gathered across from the White House once he announced the presence of the missiles in Cuba and our resolve to see them removed.

Of course, when first learning of the existence of the missiles, Kennedy could have chosen to forfeit the advantages of secrecy and **dispatch**[5] by convening a special session of Congress, requesting a declaration of war or other authorization, and adopting whatever course of action Capitol Hill's **divisive**[6] debates instructed him to pursue. But, for the technically minded, he already had one broadly worded Congressional resolution on Cuba that he had not sought, authorizing virtually anything that got tough with Castro.

But what would have been Congress's mandate had Kennedy laid the missile problem before it? His last-minute briefing of Congressional leaders produced, as starkly shown in the transcripts, only dangerous scorn for his initial package of limited responses to the new Soviet threat: the naval blockade, continuing aerial surveillance, diplomatic pressure and harsh warnings of further, unspecified American action.

To Senator William Fulbright, the chairman of the Foreign Relations Committee, a naval blockade, which could have been deemed an act of war under international law, was "the worst alternative." Far better to invade Cuba, he said, than to provoke

---

[5] **dispatch**—promptness, speed.

[6] **divisive**—tending to divide or polarize.

Moscow's retaliation by halting—or, even worse, firing upon—a Soviet vessel.

Senator Richard Russell, chairman of the Armed Services Committee, believed a war on which our very destiny hinged was "coming someday, Mr. President," and added, "Will it ever be under more **auspicious**[7] circumstances?" Like both Senator Fulbright and Senator Russell, Representative Carl Vinson, the chairman of the House Armed Services Committee, wanted to "strike with all the force and power [we possessed] and try to get it over with as quickly as possible."

That had also been the unanimous recommendation of the Joint Chiefs of Staff three days earlier. "This blockade and political action . . . will lead right into war," Gen. Curtis LeMay of the Air Force warned. "This is almost as bad as the **appeasement**[8] at Munich."[9]

It "would be considered by a lot of our friends and neutrals as being a pretty weak response to this," the general said. "And I'm sure a lot of our own citizens would feel that way, too. You're in a pretty bad fix, Mr. President."

Kennedy was indeed in a pretty bad fix. He had no good choices, no options free from the risk of either war or the erosion of our security and alliances, and no reliable forecasts on how Moscow would respond to our response. Dean Acheson, the Secretary of State under President Harry S Truman, in recommending to our group (in an untaped meeting at the State Department) an air strike against the Soviet missile sites in Cuba, acknowledged that this would then obligate the Soviets to knock out our missile complex

---

[7] **auspicious**—favorable.

[8] **appeasement**—granting concessions to potential enemies to maintain peace.

[9] Munich—an infamous 1938 meeting in the German city of Munich in which British Prime Minister Neville Chamberlain agreed to allow German annexation of the Sudetenland in exchange for Hitler's false promise of "peace in our time," as Chamberlain put it.

in Turkey, thereby obligating us to knock out a missile complex inside the Soviet Union, thereby obligating, . . . et cetera, et cetera. When Kennedy's more cautious approach succeeded, Acheson wrote the President—an **eloquent**[10] note praising his handling of the crisis. But in a magazine article several years later he said that "the Kennedys" had prevailed in this perilous situation only through "dumb luck." They were indeed lucky, I said at the time—lucky they didn't take Dean Acheson's advice.

The newly published transcripts of the first meeting of the National Security Council's Executive Committee show that virtually all of us, including the President, initially believed that at the very least an air strike against the missile sites would be necessary. And we soon learned that the only safe and sure air strike would require such a widespread bombardment of Cuba that an American invasion and occupation of that island would be an unavoidable next step. It was with this **contingency**[11] in mind that the Defense Department, at the President's instruction, began to assemble in Florida the largest American invasion force since World War II.

We now know from Soviet documents that an American military attack would have been met with fierce resistance from local Soviet troops authorized to use tactical nuclear weapons against American forces on the beaches, at sea, and in the air. Although we were less certain of that back in 1962, questions on our agenda nevertheless included the number of deaths from nuclear fallout in American cities.

So we were all lucky that week, if luck it was. We were lucky that this nation had a conventional and nuclear superiority that made Khrushchev think twice about risking an armed clash in the Western Hemisphere; lucky that,

---

[10] **eloquent**—persuasive, fluent, and graceful.
[11] **contingency**—possibility that must be prepared against.

through aerial photography and C.I.A. photo interpretation, we had enough early warning to devise in secret a response to Khrushchev's missiles that would give him an opportunity to think twice about such a clash; lucky that Kennedy had advisers like Llewellyn Thompson, the senior State Department Kremlinologist,[12] who was quietly **steadfast**[13] throughout in urging that we not force Khrushchev into a quick choice between humiliation and **escalation**.[14] We were lucky, too, that Khrushchev was statesman enough to recognize that his bold gamble had failed. And lucky, finally, that during the world's first and only (I hope) nuclear confrontation, John F. Kennedy, whose cool, prudent, prodding leadership shines through these transcript pages, was President in October 1962.

He had, after all, been elected in 1960 by only a tiny margin.

So instead of merely saying, "Well, no one was incinerated," how should I have answered the question from that religious audience in the winter of 1962–63? By what authority did Kennedy instigate his blockade and other measures? Was his action grounded in the **inherent**[15] powers of the Commander in Chief? The right of national self-defense on a nuclear-triggered planet? The moral authority of the free world leader obligated to preserve its security?

"Pick whichever makes you feel the least uncomfortable," I should have said. "The President had no choice but to lead, and he led."

I realize some philosophers and historians teach that, in the **inexorable**[16] sweep of historical tides, one person, no matter how wise or influential, cannot make a difference, cannot alter the future. In this instance, they were wrong.

---

[12] Kremlinologist—expert on the politics and power of the Soviet government. The name comes from the central Soviet government complex, the Kremlin.

[13] **steadfast**—firmly loyal, constant, and unswerving.

[14] **escalation**—intensification.

[15] **inherent**—existing as an essential part, intrinsic.

[16] **inexorable**—unchangeable.

QUESTIONS TO CONSIDER

1. What is likely to have been the result if Kennedy had put the missile crisis problem before a special session of Congress?

2. What does Sorenson believe would have happened if the U.S. had attacked the missile sites in Cuba?

3. How did the crisis finally end? What did you conclude happened?

4. In your opinion, did Kennedy act responsibly? Explain.

The Miracle Worker Annie Sullivan (right), a partially-blind orphan, rose to fame as the dedicated teacher of a deaf, mute, and blind girl, Helen Keller (left).
▼

Larger than Life

Father of U.S. Submarine Service John Phillip Holland, of County Clare, Ireland, pursued his interest in underwater transport from 1870 to 1914. After repeated failures, he built a fifty-foot-long and ten-foot-wide submarine in Elizabeth, New Jersey. The United States government bought the prototype and ordered six more.

▼

▲

A Car in Every Garage Henry Ford was the son of William Ford, an Irish Famine emigrant from County Cork. Mechanically gifted, young Henry built a machine shop and sawmill on his parents' farm near Dearborn, Michigan. He launched Ford Motor Company in 1903, and built the first Model T in 1908. He originated the assembly line technique in 1913.

PUCK.

Irish Power This 1889 *Puck* cartoon, "Cringing Before the Irish Vote," shows a horde of politicians and newspapermen paying tribute to the Irish. *Puck* published many cartoons demeaning to the Irish. They were shown as slow-witted, lazy, and un-American, and as Irish voters increased in number, a new trait was added—too powerful.

Machine Politician George Washington Plunkitt was an Irish-American leader who helped himself to political spoils. Plunkitt worked for the New York City Democratic political machine, Tammany Hall, for forty-five years.

Kennedy's Inauguration When John F. Kennedy was sworn in as President on January 20, 1961, Irish Americans felt proud and relieved. Kennedy had been forced to confront the issue of his Catholicism during the campaign, saying: "I believe in an America that is officially neither Catholic, Protestant nor Jewish . . . where the separation of church and state is absolute."

▲
Saving Lost Boys Father Edward Joseph Flanagan of County Roscommon, Ireland, served as a priest in the diocese of Omaha, Nebraska. He became concerned about the plight of homeless boys in the area and founded a home, known as Boys Town, in 1917. A popular movie about his work starred Irish Americans Spencer Tracy and Mickey Rooney.

Prose, Poetry, Songs, and Stereotypes

from

Angela's Ashes

BY FRANK McCOURT

The Irish literary tradition is hundreds of years old. Without the Irish monks, said Thomas Cahill in the opening selection of this book, our world would be a world without books. Ireland's descendants in America have carried on the tradition. The most recent Irish-American storyteller of note is Frank McCourt. He was born in New York City, spent most of his childhood in Ireland, and returned to the United States when he was nineteen. For many years, he was an English teacher at Stuyvesant High School in New York City. His best-selling memoir of his childhood, Angela's Ashes (1996), was awarded the Pulitzer Prize and the National Book Critics Award and was made into a major film. McCourt begins the book this way: "My father and mother should have stayed in New York where they met and married and where I was born. Instead, they returned to Ireland when I was four, my brother, Malachy, three, the twins, Oliver and Eugene, barely one, and my sister, Margaret, dead and gone." In the excerpt below, McCourt relates an incident from his very early childhood in New York.

A year later another child was born. Angela called him Malachy after his father and gave him a middle name, Gerard, after his father's brother.

The MacNamara sisters[1] said Angela was nothing but a rabbit and they wanted nothing to do with her till she came to her senses.

Their husbands agreed.

I'm in a playground on Classon Avenue in Brooklyn with my brother, Malachy. He's two, I'm three. We're on the seesaw.

Up, down, up, down.

Malachy goes up.

I get off.

Malachy goes down. Seesaw hits the ground. He screams. His hand is on his mouth and there's blood.

Oh, God. Blood is bad. My mother will kill me.

And here she is, trying to run across the playground. Her big belly slows her.

She says, What did you do? What did you do to the child?

I don't know what to say. I don't know what I did.

She pulls my ear. Go home. Go to bed.

Bed? In the middle of the day?

She pushes me toward the playground gate. Go.

She picks up Malachy and waddles off.

My father's friend, Mr. MacAdorey, is outside our building. He's standing at the edge of the sidewalk with his wife, Minnie, looking at a dog lying in the gutter. There is blood all around the dog's head. It's the color of the blood from Malachy's mouth.

Malachy has dog blood and the dog has Malachy blood.

I pull Mr. MacAdorey's hand. I tell him Malachy has blood like the dog.

---

[1] MacNamara sisters—his mother Angela's cousins Delia and Philomena. These women are very critical. The comment about being a rabbit is a reference to how frequently rabbits have babies.

Oh, he does, indeed, Francis. Cats have it, too. And Eskimos. All the same blood.

Minnie says, Stop that, Dan. Stop confusing the wee fellow. She tells me the poor wee dog was hit by a car and he crawled all the way from the middle of the street before he died. Wanted to come home, the poor wee creature.

Mr. MacAdorey says, You'd better go home, Francis. I don't know what you did to your wee brother, but your mother took him off to the hospital. Go home, child.

Will Malachy die like the dog, Mr. MacAdorey?

Minnie says, He bit his tongue. He won't die.

Why did the dog die?

It was his time, Francis.

The apartment is empty and I wander between the two rooms, the bedroom and the kitchen. My father is out looking for a job and my mother is at the hospital with Malachy. I wish I had something to eat but there's nothing in the icebox but cabbage leaves floating in the melted ice. My father said never eat anything floating in water for the rot that might be in it. I fall asleep on my parents' bed and when my mother shakes me it's nearly dark. Your little brother is going to sleep a while. Nearly bit his tongue off. Stitches galore. Go into the other room.

My father is in the kitchen sipping black tea from his big white enamel mug. He lifts me to his lap.

Dad, will you tell me the story about Coo Coo?

Cuchulain. Say it after me, Coo-hoo-lin. I'll tell you the story when you say the name right. Coo-hoo-lin.

I say it right and he tells me the story of Cuchulain, who had a different name when he was a boy, Setanta. He grew up in Ireland where Dad lived when he was a boy in County Antrim. Setanta had a stick and ball and one day he hit the ball and it went into the mouth of a big dog that belonged to Culain and choked him. Oh, Culain was angry and he said, What am I to do now without my big dog to guard my house and my wife and my ten small children as well as numerous pigs, hens, sheep?

Setanta said, I'm sorry. I'll guard your house with my stick and ball and I'll change my name to Cuchulain, the Hound of Culain. He did. He guarded the house and regions beyond and became a great hero, the Hound of Ulster itself. Dad said he was a greater hero than Hercules or Achilles that the Greeks were always bragging about and he could take on King Arthur and all his knights in a fair fight which, of course, you could never get with an Englishman anyway.

That's my story. Dad can't tell that story to Malachy or any other children down the hall.

He finishes the story and lets me sip his tea. It's bitter, but I'm happy there on his lap.

For days Malachy's tongue is swollen and he can hardly make a sound never mind talk. But even if he could no one is paying any attention to him because we have two new babies who were brought by an angel in the middle of the night. The neighbors say, Ooh, Ah, they're lovely boys, look at those big eyes.

Malachy stands in the middle of the room, looking up at everyone, pointing to his tongue and saying, Uck, uck. When the neighbors say, Can't you see we're looking at your little brothers? he cries, till Dad pats him on the head. Put in your tongue, son, and go out and play with Frankie. Go on.

In the playground I tell Malachy about the dog who died in the street because someone drove a ball into his mouth. Malachy shakes his head. No uck ball. Car uck kill dog. He cries because his tongue hurts and he can hardly talk and it's terrible when you can't talk. He won't let me push him on the swing. He says, You uck kill me uck on seesaw. He gets Freddie Leibowitz to push him and he's happy, laughing when he swings to the sky. Freddie is big, he's seven, and I ask him to push me. He says, No, you tried to kill your brother.

I try to get the swing going myself but all I can do is move it back and forth and I'm angry because Freddie and Malachy are laughing at the way I can't swing. They're great pals now, Freddie, seven, Malachy, two. They laugh every day and Malachy's tongue gets better with all the laughing.

When he laughs you can see how white and small and pretty his teeth are and you can see his eyes shine. He has blue eyes like my mother. He has golden hair and pink cheeks. I have brown eyes like Dad. I have black hair and my cheeks are white in the mirror. My mother tells Mrs. Leibowitz down the hall that Malachy is the happiest child in the world. She tells Mrs. Leibowitz down the hall, Frankie has the odd manner like his father. I wonder what the odd manner is but I can't ask because I'm not supposed to be listening.

I wish I could swing up into the sky, up into the clouds. I might be able to fly around the whole world and not hear my brothers, Oliver and Eugene, cry in the middle of the night anymore. My mother says they're always hungry. She cries in the middle of the night, too. She says she's worn out nursing and feeding and changing and four boys is too much for her. She wishes she had one little girl all for herself. She'd give anything for one little girl.

I'm in the playground with Malachy. I'm four, he's three. He lets me push him on the swing because he's no good at swinging himself and Freddie Leibowitz is in school. We have to stay in the playground because the twins are sleeping and my mother says she's worn out. Go out and play, she says, and give me some rest. Dad is out looking for a job again and sometimes he comes home with the smell of whiskey, singing all the songs about suffering Ireland. Mam gets angry and says Ireland can kiss her arse. He says that's nice language to be using in front of the children and she says never mind the language, food on the table is what she wants, not suffering Ireland. She says it was a sad day Prohibition ended because Dad gets the drink going around to saloons offering to sweep out the bars and lift barrels for a whiskey or a beer. Sometimes he brings home bits of the free lunch, rye bread, corned beef, pickles. He puts the food on the table and drinks tea himself. He says food is a shock to the system and he doesn't know where we get our appetites. Mam says, They get their appetites because they're starving half the time.

QUESTIONS TO CONSIDER

1. What words would you use to describe Frankie's feelings toward his brother Malachy?

2. What does the incident about the dog that was hit by a car add to the story? Why do you think it was included?

3. What are the issues surrounding Frankie's father? What are Frankie's feelings toward his father?

4. How is Ireland important to this story?

The High Divers

BY JACK CONROY

Irish-American author Jack Conroy (1898-1990) was born near Moberly, Missouri, at the old Monkey Nest Coal Mine site. His short stories often focused on the lives of working-class people. Conroy befriended struggling young writers and some of America's literary greats are among those he helped—Richard Wright, Erskine Caldwell, Nelson Algren, Tom McGrath. In the following tale he echoes the exaggeration and humor characteristic of the traditional tall tales of Irish folklore.

You ask me why I'm bunged up this way, going on crutches, both arms busted and what may still be a fractured skull. The doc ain't sure about that yet. I'll live, I guess, but I don't know what for. I can't never be a high diver no more. I'll go to selling razor blades, like as not, and there's plenty doing that already.

Eddie La Breen is to blame for it all. High diving was an easy and high-paying profession before he tried to root me and every other performer out[1] of it. I would

---

[1] root . . .out—dig up by the roots; totally remove.

go traveling in the summer with a carnival and my high dive would be a free feature attraction. The local merchants would kick in for signs to put on my ladder and advertise their goods. Sometimes I'd make a little **spiel**[2] from the top of the ladder just before I dived off into the tank.

Eddie La Breen called himself the "Human Seal." He bragged that he could dive higher into shallower water than any man alive. I was pretty good myself, being billed as Billie, the Dolphin, Spectacular and Deathdefying High Diver Extraordinary.

I'm doing all right with Miller's Great Exposition Shows, using a twenty-five foot ladder and diving into a ten foot tank. Big crowds of people would come from miles around to see me and not a soul ever seemed dissatisfied until we happened to be playing Omaha on a lot over ten blocks away from where Eddie La Breen is Playing with Baker's World's Fair Show. Just when I come up out of the tank and start to take a bow one night, I hear somebody say: "That ain't nothing. You ought to see Eddie La Breen over on Farnum Street diving twice as high into water half as deep."

I found out it's so. Eddie has been diving into five feet of water from a fifty foot ladder, and Mr. Miller threatens to let me go if I can't do as well.

It sure looked high when I got up there and I could feel my nose scraping on the bottom of the tank just as I made the upturn. But I'm no slouch[3] at the high dive myself, and Eddie La Breen ain't going to outdo me if I can help it.

I added the fire act to my dive, too, and most of the time I could hardly see where to dive. For the fire act you have a little bit of gasoline pouring into the tank. It stays right on top of the water and when you fire it, it makes a fearful sight, splashing fire in every direction when you hit the water.

---

[2] **spiel**—short speech intended to advertise a product or service.

[3] no slouch—not an awkward, lazy, or inept person; not an amateur.

Eddie sends me word that I might as well give up. "I'm going to dive next from a thousand feet into a tank of solid concrete," he says, "and I'll do it while playing the ukulele,[4] eating raw liver, and keeping perfect time. Why, when I was a kid of ten, I could dive off a silo into dew in the grass, bellybuster, and never even grunt when I lit."[5]

He didn't quite do what he said, but he did enough. He raised his ladder to a hundred feet, and kept only two and a half feet of water in the tank.

I practiced and practiced and got a few bruises, but I cut that depth to two feet and raised my ladder to a hundred and fifty feet.

By this time Eddie sent word he was good and mad, and he's going to call himself the Minnow. "You know how a minnow just skitters along on top of a pond," he says. "Well, that's the way I'll light on that tank. From two hundred feet I'll dive into six inches of water and just skim off without hardly making a bubble."

If ever a man practiced hard to make a shallow dive, that was me. I did that minnow dive in four inches of water from a height of two hundred fifty feet, lit right on my feet after barely touching the water, and didn't even muss my hair.

When Eddie makes it from three hundred feet into three inches, I'm a little put out, but I don't give up. I tell Miller to get me a good heavy bath mat and soak it good all day. First time I hit that mat it sort of knocked me dizzy. You know how it is when you have the breath knocked out of you and all you can do is croak like a frog. But I got better and better at it until I hardly puffed at all.

I beat Eddie La Breen fair and square but he wasn't man enough to take it or admit it like a man. He showed

---

[4] ukulele—stringed instrument like a small guitar.

[5] lit—landed.

that he was rotten to the core and treacherous from the word go.

We were playing Sheboygan, Wisconsin, and I had no idea that Eddie was anywhere within miles. I had heard that Barker had told him to pack up and get out when I bested him.

When I hit that bath mat that night, I thought my time had come. That was six months ago, and look at me now. Still on crutches and lucky if I ever get off of them.

Well, sir, I don't know anybody but Eddie who wanted to do me dirt.[6] They had soaked my heavy bath mat in water all day the same as usual, but they must have let it get out of their sight sometime or other, because somebody had wrung it out practically dry.

That's the way I had it. I heard somebody say later that a man answering the description of Eddie La Breen had been seen lurking around the show grounds that evening. And if he didn't do it, who did?

---

[6] do me dirt—hurt me.

QUESTIONS TO CONSIDER

1. How is exaggeration used for emphasis or effect in this short story?

2. Why does the narrator blame his accident on Eddie LaBreen? Does the story context make you believe that Eddie is responsible for the accident?

3. What folk tales does this story remind you of? Why?

Cagney and Cohan: Irish-American Symbols

BY WILLIAM D. GRIFFIN

Historian Griffin compares two legendary Irish Americans from show business—George M. Cohan and James Cagney. Cohan was born on July 3, 1878, the grandson of Irish Famine immigrants from County Cork. George grew up as a child of the Irish musical stage. With his parents and sister, he toured in early vaudeville as part of the "Four Cohans." He began composing songs for the family productions and wrote himself the lead in his own Broadway plays in the 1901–1932 period, when he became an enormous star. Audiences loved Cohan's patriotic songs, but highbrow critics never warmed to him. James Cagney—who won an Academy Award for portraying Cohan in the film Yankee Doodle Dandy—*grew up on the East Side of New York City, the son of a saloon-keeper. One of seven children, he originally wanted to be a farmer. Needing a job, however, he turned to the theater. A stage manager trained him to sing, dance, and do female impressions. Cagney went on to have an extraordinary film career, both in musical and dramatic roles, often playing tough guys and gangsters.*

When James Cagney died in 1986, one also thought of George M. Cohan, who had died forty-four years earlier. The mental connection was inevitable, for the two were perpetually linked by Cagney's portrayal of Cohan in the film biography "Yankee Doodle Dandy." Cagney had won an Academy Award for his performance as the flag-waving showman in a year—1942—when patriotic fervor was at its highest. Cagney, who had also been a song-and-dance man in his earlier days, was an appropriate choice for the part and gave an outstanding performance. But, actually, the two men had little in common, aside from their Irish background, and their entertainment careers followed very different patterns. Indeed, the images that they projected as performers made them symbols in the public minds of two different types—perhaps the only types—of Irish Americans.

Cohan was active in show business for most of his life (1878–1942), first as a member of a family vaudeville troupe, then, from 1901, as author, director, and producer of a long string of successful Broadway musical comedies. In the characters he created—and often played—Cohan became the **quintessential**[1] "Irishman" for millions of Americans—**amiable**,[2] cheerful, always ready with a smile or tear, always prepared to burst into a sentimental song and raise a convivial cup. This lighthearted, if somewhat light-weight, character was proud of his origins: like "Harrigan," he was "proud of all the Irish blood that's in me." His loyalties, however, very definitely lay on this side of the Atlantic. With songs such as "Over There," "You're a Grand Old Flag," and, of course "I'm a Yankee Doodle Dandy," he emphasized the 110 percent patriotism of the Irish-American. And— patriotism aside—what could be more American than

---

[1] **quintessential**—purest, most highly concentrated essence of something.

[2] **amiable**—good-natured, friendly.

"Give My Regards to Broadway"? This **potentate**[3] of the popular stage ventured only once into the realm of "serious" theater then dominated by his fellow Celt, Eugene O'Neill, when he played the father in "Ah, Wilderness!" (1932).

It was during this period, when Cohan stood at the **pinnacle**[4] of his career as a stage entertainer, that Cagney was beginning his, as a film performer. During the 1930s he starred in a series of gangster films, of which *Public Enemy* is the most famous. These established him in the minds of moviegoers as the street-wise Irish tough guy—cocky, self-confident, aggressive, always ready with a snarl or a blow. His role in "The Fighting 69th" (1940) took him off the streets and into uniform, but kept him in character. Even the totally different assignment he received in "Yankee Doodle Dandy" failed to permanently alter the Jimmy Cagney of popular imagination. (Cohan, who had recommended Cagney for the role, saw the film a few months before his death and was greatly impressed by the actor's talent as a song-and-dance man; Cagney called Cohan "the real leader of our clan.")

Cagney made many films during the twenty-odd years after the Cohan tribute. Although he played everything from an American agent in occupied France to a rancher in the Old West, not to mention an Irish revolutionary in 1920s Dublin ("Shake Hands with the Devil"), it was his "Public Enemy" **persona**[5] that endured. It was fitting, therefore, that when he came out of retirement in the early 1970s to do a cameo role[6] in "Ragtime" it was to play Inspector Thomas Byrnes. Although the part was a brief one, arranged to accommodate Cagney's age and poor health, he

---

[3] **potentate**—one who dominates or leads.

[4] **pinnacle**—highest point.

[5] **persona**—character; role.

[6] cameo role—small part that showcases a famous actor.

seemed back in character as a real-life turn-of-the-century New York police official with a reputation for **ruthlessness**[7] and playing both sides of the law.

Between them, Cagney and Cohan **epitomized**[8] the Irish-American for most of their fellow countrymen during the first half of the twentieth century. The screen actor was the tough "Mick," the stage actor, the **genial**[9] "Pat." Both images embodied favorable and unfavorable elements. The Cagney type was admirable in his **brash**[10] self-assertiveness, but it helped preserve the "Irish gangster" cliches that only gradually yielded to those of the "Italian gangster." The Cohan type was **convivial**[11] and charming, but it suggested the shallow emotionalism and reinforced the idea of the "drinking Irish" just as Cagney suggested the "fighting Irish."

From the birth of Cohan to the death of Cagney stretches a span of 108 years. At its beginning, the Irish were still the **alien**,[12] excluded objects of contempt and hostility. By its end, they have become the most **assimilated**[13] and the most successful of all immigrant groups. The images that Cagney and Cohan conveyed have now yielded to a variety of life-styles, occupations, and attitudes too varied to encompass in one or two stock characters. Were those images stereotypes? It seems better to call them symbols marking an intermediate stage from the stereotypical Irish of the nineteenth century to the assimilated Irish of the twenty-first.

---

[7] **ruthlessness**—tending to act without compassion or pity.

[8] **epitomized**—typified.

[9] **genial**—friendly or pleasant.

[10] **brash**—hasty and unthinking; rash.

[11] **convivial**—sociable; jovial.

[12] **alien**—belonging to another country; unfamiliar; strange.

[13] **assimilated**—absorbed into the larger society or culture.

QUESTIONS TO CONSIDER

1. What are the two Irish stereotypes embodied in Cagney and Cohan?

2. How are those two symbols still associated with Irish Americans today?

3. When ethnic stereotypes disappear, who or what takes their place?

Immigrant Daughter's Song

BY MARY ANN LARKIN

Contemporary Irish-American poets, singers, and writers continue to create works that describe the emotional landscape of the Irish Famine and the Irish immigrant experience. Mary Ann Larkin is a poet, teacher, editor, development consultant, and writer who was born in 1945. She was a founding member of a performing group of women poets, the Big Mama Poetry Troupe, and published her first book of poetry, The Coil of the Skin, *in 1982. Her work appears in many anthologies. Larkin has given poetry workshops and readings in colleges, churches, jails, saloons, and schools. She lives in Washington, D.C.*

All gone,
the silver-green silk of time
winding down centuries
of custom and kinship
the pouring of the sea
the stars, bright pictures
on the slate of night,
the moon stamping forever
the spire of the church
on the sand,
bird-song, wind-song, mother-song
Even time itself changed
to a ticking, a dot on a line

Customs of grace and gentleness gone
name-saying
and knowing
who begat who
and when and where
and who could work
and who could sing
and who would pray
and who would not
and where the fish ran
and the wild plums hid
and how the old mothers
fit their babies' fingers
to the five-flowered hollows
of blue ladyfingers
And whose father fought whose
with golden swords
a thousand years ago
at Ballyferriter
on the strand below the church

All gone
changed from a silken spool unwinding
to rooms of relics and loss
behind whose locked doors
I dream
not daring to wake

QUESTIONS TO CONSIDER

1. What feeling is evoked as the "Immigrant Daughter" looks back to Ireland?

2. How does the poet's use of dream images, like the "pouring of the sea and stars" and "a silken spool unwinding," permit readers to imagine a world that never existed for them? Why are the concrete details of the lost world necessary for evoking a "dream"?

3. Why do you think the poet is behind "locked doors"?

Mark O'Brien, Journalist and Poet in an Iron Lung

BY WILLIAM H. HONAN

Mark O'Brien, the disabled Irish-American poet and writer who died in 1999, inspired many people with disabilities to pursue their interests and their careers regardless of their physical limitations. The Center for Independent Living in Berkeley, California, where he lived, drew disabled people from around the country who wanted to challenge themselves and their need for assisted living. Many of those who were confined to wheelchairs felt themselves more capable and free when they saw Mark traveling the streets of Berkeley on his electric gurney, and he opened doors for more disabled who sought admission to the university. The following is from his obituary in The New York Times.

Mark O'Brien, the subject of an Academy Award-winning documentary about his journalism career, conducted mostly from an iron lung, died on July 4 at his home in Berkeley, Calif. He was 49.

The cause was complications from **bronchitis**,[1] said Mr. O'Brien's brother, Kenneth.

The 1997 film "Breathing Lessons: The Life and Work of Mark O'Brien," directed by Jessica Yu, described his struggle to live productively with minimal assistance and his determination to live on his own and work. He also founded a publishing company.

Months of declining health had kept Mr. O'Brien dependent on the iron lung for all but a few hours a week, his friends said.

Mr. O'Brien, who was born in Boston and reared in Sacramento, Calif., was a boy when polio left him paralyzed from the neck down and forced him to use the iron lung.

At some times in his youth, and for a brief period as recently as last year, Mr. O'Brien's breathing could be supported by an inflatable vest called a turtle shell. But for most of his life he depended on the much more **cumbersome**[2] iron lung, which encased most of his body and helped him breathe by changing the pressure around him.

About one hundred polio survivors in the United States are using iron lungs.

Mr. O'Brien enrolled at the University of California at Berkeley in 1978. He became a familiar figure on the streets of Berkeley, navigating his electric gurney[3] on trips between the campus and the tiny apartment where he kept his iron lung. In 1982, he received a bachelor's degree in English literature.

After repeated applications, Mr. O'Brien was admitted to the Graduate School of Journalism at Berkeley. His acceptance set a **precedent**[4] that helped other severely disabled applicants to state universities.

---

[1] **bronchitis**—chronic or acute inflammation of the bronchial tubes.

[2] **cumbersome**—clumsy, unwieldy, burdensome.

[3] electric gurney—a motorized, wheeled stretcher.

[4] **precedent**—example for dealing with similar cases.

His work was first published in 1979, when *Co-Evolution Quarterly* printed his essay on independent living. Sandy Close, executive editor of Pacific News Service, saw the article and hired Mr. O'Brien as a correspondent. Mr. Close later produced "Breathing Lessons."

Mr. Close said Mr. O'Brien initially dictated his articles, then used a stick in his mouth to press the keys of an I.B.M. Selectric typewriter and finally employed a word processor.

In 1997, Mr. O'Brien co-founded Lemonade Factory, a small press in Berkeley that publishes poetry by people with disabilities.

Mr. O'Brien, who said his strong Roman Catholic faith helped him cope with his disability, had two great passions besides writing: baseball and Shakespeare.

In addition to his brother, Kenneth, of Granite Bay, Calif., he is survived by his father, Walter F., also of Granite Bay, and a sister, Rachel Jordan, of Weimar, Calif.

Mr. O'Brien published several volumes of poetry, including a collection called "Breathing," which included the following lines:

This most excellent canopy,[5] the air, look you,
Presses down upon me
At fifteen pounds per square inch,
A dense, heavy, blue glowing ocean,
Supporting the weight of condors[6]
That swim its churning currents.
All I get is a thin stream of it,
A finger's width of the rope that ties me to life
As I labor like a stevedore[7] to keep the connection.

---

[5] *canopy*—any high covering, in this case the sky.

[6] *condors*—large sea birds, vultures.

[7] *stevedore*—laborer who loads and unloads ships.

QUESTIONS TO CONSIDER

1. How does the fact that Mark used a stick in his mouth to write the poem affect your interpretation? Should it?

2. How would you feel if you saw a person on an electric gurney coming down a sidewalk? Why?

3. What message does it send when a person with serious disabilities goes on to accomplish something that would be difficult for a fully functioning person?

4. What challenges and rewards await people who take their disabilities public?

▲

Roaring Twenties F. Scott Fitzgerald, the descendant of southern colonial landowners and Irish immigrants, was twenty-two years old when his first novel, *This Side of Paradise,* was published. He married Zelda Sayre the same year. Scott and Zelda were a beautiful and famous couple, but their self-destructive lifestyle mirrored that of the rich, sophisticated, and disillusioned young people portrayed in Fitzgerald's novels, *Tender Is the Night, The Last Tycoon,* and his masterpiece, *The Great Gatsby.*

A Touch of the Poet Eugene O'Neill, the grandson of Irish immigrants, is one of America's most famous dramatists. He won the Pulitzer Prize four times and was named the 1936 Nobel laureate in literature. His greatest plays include, *Long Day's Journey into Night, The Iceman Cometh,* and *Moon for the Misbegotten.* ▶

Requiem for an Irish Family There are few happy scenes like this from O'Neill's biographical play, *Long Day's Journey Into Night.* The fictional Tyrone family acts out the O'Neills' harrowing real-life experiences. Eugene's mother, Ella Quinlan O'Neill, had become addicted to morphine, and the emotional consequences for the family were devastating.
▼

▲

Courting Fame Brothers Malachy (left) and Frank McCourt both achieved literary fame in America. Malachy's best-selling memoir, *A Monk Swimming,* chronicles his family's immigration to America. Frank's Pulitzer Prize-winning memoir, *Angela's Ashes,* chronicles his impoverished childhood in Ireland.

▲
Anna Quindlen This Irish-American columnist and novelist won a Pulitzer Prize in 1992. Her novel *One True Thing* was made into a movie in 1998.

James Cagney Growing up poor on New York's lower East Side, Cagney found theater work on Broadway. He became one of film's most famous gangsters in *Public Enemy* (1931) and went on to play the tough guy in *Angels with Dirty Faces, Smart Money,* and many others. He broke out of his gangster role and won an Oscar for Best Male Actor in 1942 when he played the Irish dancer, songwriter, and singer George M. Cohan in *Yankee Doodle Dandy,* shown here. ▶

Cinematic Genius Film director John Ford was born Sean O'Feeney, the youngest of thirteen children, in 1895. He achieved recognition as one of America's most accomplished directors with *The Grapes of Wrath, Young Mr. Lincoln, The Searchers, Stagecoach,* and *The Fugitive.* He directed several films with Irish themes, including *The Informer, The Quiet Man,* and *The Rising of the Moon.* He won four Academy Awards.

◄ **Grace Kelly** Born into a wealthy
Philadelphia family with Irish roots, Kelly
became a successful model and an actress.
She achieved international recognition for her
starring roles in eleven films, including three
Alfred Hitchcock directed thrillers: *Rear
Window, Dial M for Murder,* and *To Catch a
Thief.* She also starred in *High Noon* and won
an Academy Award for her performance in
The Country Girl. She gave up acting to marry
Prince Rainier of Monaco, and died in a car
crash in 1982.

Baseball Dreams John McGraw, son of poor Irish immigrants, lost his mother and three sisters to diphtheria when he was twelve. He became a $40-a-month baseball player at seventeen, and player-manager for the Baltimore Orioles in the 1890s. He developed the inside game of baseball strategy—the bunt, the steal, and the hit-and-run. He took over the New York Giants in 1902, and his teams won ten National League championships and three World Series titles. ▶

Connie Mack Cornelius McGillicuddy became a factory worker after elementary school but went on to become a major figure in American baseball. As a manager, he won nine American League pennants and five World Series titles. He was elected to the Baseball Hall of Fame in 1938.

The Manassa Mauler Jack Dempsey, the boxing champion and national hero of the 1920s, left his Manassa, Colorado, home at the age of sixteen. In 1919, he knocked out Jess Willard to become the heavyweight champion. His tremendous skill was memorialized in this painting by George Bellows. He is shown being knocked out of the ring by Angel Louis Firpo, an extraordinary moment in the fight. Helped back into the ring, Dempsey fought on and won.

▼

Women in the Ring Irish lightweight boxer Dierdre Gogarty moved to Dublin at age 19 to study boxing. She later moved to the United States, where she started training with former heavyweight champion Beau Williford.

▼

Irish Americans
at the Millennium

The Black
and the Green

BY BRIAN DOOLEY

The Irish and African Americans have both suffered from prejudice and discrimination. In 1860, the British humor magazine Punch *claimed that both the Irish and the Negro were at the bottom of the evolutionary ladder. In 1890, the London Zoo named their new chimpanzee "Paddy" to general amusement among the English. Irish Famine immigrants to America were called "White Negroes" and "Negroes turned inside out." Blacks were referred to as "smoked Irish." Brian Dooley, an Irish American himself, is director of communications for Public Citizen, a Washington, D.C.-based consumer advocacy group. His book,* Black and Green: The Fight for Civil Rights in Northern Ireland and Black America, *was published in London in 1998. In it he explains the historic connections between the two groups in their struggles against oppression.*

Exactly thirty years ago this October, the Northern Ireland civil rights movement burst onto the international scene when television pictures showed marchers being **batoned**[1] off the streets of Derry by the police.

Non-violent protests against discrimination had been **percolating**[2] for years, but it was the small march in Derry that really launched the movement. When film showed the police using water cannon against the marchers, commentators all over the world compared the scene to black civil rights marches in the U.S., an identification the marchers themselves were keen to encourage.

Like the black American activists, they demanded an end to **gerrymandering**,[3] fair housing distribution and "One Man, One Vote," and sang "We Shall Overcome" at rallies, sit-ins and marches across Northern Ireland.

They called themselves Ulster's White Negroes, and drew on the historic connection between black American civil rights activists and Irish nationalists.

The links went back for several centuries. In the mid-1600s, Oliver Cromwell's English army invaded Ireland and banished many Irish to become slaves in the West Indies, where some worked side by side with black slaves in Caribbean sugar cane fields. In Bermuda in 1661 and Barbados in 1668 the Irish on the islands were suspected of collaborating with black slaves in planning insurrection against the British authorities. The small Caribbean island of Montserrat became particularly closely identified with Ireland, and a 1780 book recorded that the vast majority of the inhabitants were either descendants of the original Irish settlers or natives of Ireland, "so that the use of the Irish language is preserved on the island, even among the Negroes."

Ties were strengthened in the mid-nineteenth century, when Daniel O'Connell publicly condemned American

---

[1] **batoned**—hit with batons, or nightsticks.

[2] **percolating**—bubbling up.

[3] **gerrymandering**—the division of voting districts in order to give unfair advantage to one party or race.

slavery. In 1845, former slave Frederick Douglass toured Ireland to rouse support for the campaign to abolish slavery in America, and appeared with O'Connell at a political rally in Dublin's Liberty Hall.

Douglass witnessed the **destitution**[4] of many Irish peasants—his visit coincided with the first year of the Famine—and was struck by the similarities to Southern slaves.

After addressing a huge meeting in Cork, Douglass wrote: "Never did human faces tell a sadder tale. More than five thousand were assembled . . . these people lacked only a black skin and woolly hair to complete their likeness to the plantation negro. The open, uneducated mouth—the long gaunt arm—the badly formed foot and ankle—the shuffling gait . . . all reminded me of the plantation, and my own cruelly abused people."

Throughout Douglass's rise to the top levels of the U.S. Government—eventually becoming Minister to Haiti—he vigorously championed Irish independence, calling for an end to British rule, and hosting receptions in Washington D.C. for visiting Irish MPs.[5]

The black American-Irish connection was strengthened in the early years of this century by Marcus Garvey, the political grandfather of black nationalism—who modeled the organization of his Universal Negro Improvement Association on the structure of Sinn Féin.[6] At the month-long UNIA rally at Madison Square Garden in August 1920, Garvey telegrammed Eamon de Valera in the name of twenty-five thousand black delegates to formally recognize him as president of the Irish Republic, and that same year Garvey sent repeated messages of support to IRA hunger striker Terence MacSwiney.

---

[4] **destitution**—extreme poverty.

[5] MPs—members of the British Parliament.

[6] Sinn Féin—the political arm of the Irish Republican Army (IRA), a paramilitary group that opposes British rule in Northern Ireland.

By the early 1960s, the black American struggle was again providing inspiration and support for Irish activists. The **fledgling**[7] anti-discrimination movements in Northern Ireland repeated the sit-in and marching tactics of Martin Luther King, and borrowed some of the more radical strategies of black student organizations.

Northern Ireland civil rights leaders like Michael Farrell carefully studied the black American movement, and in the tense months following the Derry march of October 5, 1968, deliberately copied its methods of exposing government violence.

Farrell was prominent in People's Democracy, the student movement that had sprung up around Queen's University, Belfast, in the days after the Derry march. He led a civil rights march from Belfast to Derry in January 1969 that was carefully modeled on the black civil rights march from Selma to Montgomery [Alabama] of 1965. "The Selma–Montgomery march forced the federal government to intervene in Alabama. . . the local law enforcement agency was completely biased against blacks, and you could not achieve any sort of justice within the legal institutional or political structures within Alabama, so they staged a dramatic march across Alabama which was attacked by white racists," argued Farrell.

The Belfast–Derry march turned out to be no less dramatic. The young protesters sang "On To Selma" as they walked, in conscious imitation of black American marchers. They were violently attacked by hundreds of counter-demonstrators at Burntollet and (like in Alabama) the local police refused to protect the civil rights demonstrators.

The police inaction at Burntollet made comparisons with Alabama all the more obvious, and undermined the credibility of the Northern Ireland government—precisely the result Farrell had been hoping for.

---

[7] **fledgling**—young and inexperienced.

Links between the student protesters in Northern Ireland and the radical elements of the American movement were cemented later that year when Eilis McDermott of People's Democracy visited Black Panther[8] headquarters in New York and was made an "honorary Panther."

Nineteen sixty nine also saw Bernadette Devlin's[9] first visit to the U.S. Spirited out of Derry as British troops arrived to end the Battle of the Bogside in August, she arrived in America to give an eyewitness account of the fighting between police and Catholic residents of the Bogside, and to raise money for the civil rights effort in Northern Ireland.

Devlin [later Bernadette McAliskey] was a 22-year-old student at Queen's in Belfast, the most prominent activist in People's Democracy, and had been elected to the British parliament for the mid-Ulster constituency in April 1969 on a civil rights platform.

An undeniably articulate and engaging personality, Devlin became an instant hit with the U.S. media, appeared on major TV shows across the country, and won a wider audience for the Northern Ireland civil rights campaign than all previous visiting spokespeople combined.

Apart from speaking at the usual round of Irish-American clubs and political meetings, Devlin also visited Operation Bootstrap in Watts, the black district of Los Angeles torn apart by riots a few years earlier. Devlin disturbed many of her Irish American hosts by pointedly reminding them that if they supported civil rights in Ireland, they should also support them in the U.S.

Four days into the trip, she astonished an Irish-American rally in Philadelphia when she sang—even danced—with a black man, and asked him to sing "We Shall Overcome" to the audience. When presented with

---

[8] Black Panther—referring to the radical African-American political party active in the Civil Rights Movement of the 1960s.

[9] Bernadette Devlin's—pertaining to the fiery opponent of British rule in Northern Ireland who won election to the British Parliament's House of Commons.

the keys of New York City by Mayor John Lindsay, she promptly had them turned over to the local Black Panther Party as a gesture of support for their efforts. Her vocal criticism of Chicago Mayor Richard Daley's handling of New Left protests at the Democratic Convention the previous summer alarmed many Irish Americans, and her popularity in conservative circles rapidly dwindled.

"Those who were supposed to be 'my people,' the Irish Americans who knew about English misrule and the famine and supported the civil rights movement at home . . . looked and sounded to me like Orangemen.[10] They said exactly the same things about blacks that the Loyalists said about us at home," she said.

In Detroit she **admonished**[11] Irish-Americans for refusing "to stand shoulder to shoulder with their fellow black Americans," and the trip ended in confusion when Devlin became increasingly suspicious that the funds she was raising were to be used to buy guns. She had specifically told audiences that she did not want the money for guns, but had overheard an organizer of her trip suggesting that the dollars might be diverted for arms anyway. Devlin cut short her trip, refusing to go to Boston or Washington, D.C., to ask people for money when she could not guarantee how it might be used.

She returned to the U.S. in February 1971, and the conservative Irish-Americans who now stayed away from her appearances were being replaced by black Americans as word spread of her interest in the civil rights struggle in the U.S. During the trip she met prominent radical black leaders like Huey P. Newton and Stokeley Carmichael and—despite strenuous objections from the local Irish-American community in San Francisco—even visited Angela Davis in prison.

---

[10] Orangemen—Protestants in Northern Ireland who favor the continuation of British rule there.
[11] **admonished**—found fault with.

Davis had been on the FBI's "Ten Most Wanted" list, been publicly identified by President Richard Nixon as a "terrorist" and was awaiting trial for murder and kidnapping when Devlin visited her. "Angela Davis and I are involved in the same struggle . . . for the liberation of our own people," said Devlin after the visit. (Davis was acquitted of all charges.)

Devlin confronted Irish-Americans with the **ambiguity**[12] of supporting civil rights on one side of the Atlantic and not the other.

Relations between Irish-Americans and blacks have been complicated and, at times, even violent. In the mid-1800s, newly-arrived Irish immigrants often competed with freed black Americans for jobs, and the two groups shared a similar social status. American employers in the middle of the nineteenth century often had their pick of Irish or black labor. In his study of the American slave system in the 1850s, Frederick Law Olmsted recorded that some preferred Irish workers, others black.

One Virginia landowner claimed Irish workers would perform over 50 per cent more work in a day than black slaves; another tobacco farmer from the same state explained to Olmsted that he employed Irish laborers over blacks not because they were more productive ("he thought a negro could do twice as much work, in a day, as an Irishman") but because the work could be dangerous, and "a negro's life is too valuable to be risked at it. If a negro dies, it's a considerable loss, you know," Olmsted was told.

Whatever their relative merits, black and Irish workers were commonly regarded as comprising the lowest social strata of American society. An English historian visiting the U.S. wrote home in 1881: "This would be a grand land if only every Irishman would kill a Negro,

---

[12] **ambiguity**—confused meaning.

and be hanged for it. I find this sentiment generally approved—sometimes with the qualification that they want Irish and Negroes for servants, not being able to get any other."

The sense of persecution shared by black Americans and Irish immigrants did not always lead to solidarity between the two groups. Violence broke out in several North American cities as freed blacks competed with Irish laborers in the job market, and black Americans were famous for telling "Irish jokes" during the 1800s, as laughing at Irish immigrants was one of the few ways that black Americans could openly take revenge on whites. To make fun of white Americans was not acceptable, but to join in the laughter at the Irish was. In 1876 one writer noted that black stevedores working in Cincinnati "can mimic the Irish accent to a degree of perfection which an American, Englishman, or German could not hope to acquire."

The Irish featured in the jokes told by blacks are characterized by their stupidity and laziness. One told of an Irishman who bought a gun and immediately killed his friend by trying to shoot the grasshopper on his chest, another of the Irishman who bought a watermelon and only ate the rind.

During the twentieth century, the perception of Irish-American hostility towards blacks has often been rooted more in reputation than fact, although the Clann Na Gael branch in Philadelphia only agreed to carry a civil rights banner during the 1969 St. Patrick's Day parade on condition it clearly supported civil rights in Northern Ireland, not black civil rights in the U.S. . . .

Other Irish-Americans were more supportive of the black struggle. The late Paul O'Dwyer, for example, represented American blacks in civil rights cases and was involved with black political campaigns in Mississippi. O'Dwyer also wrote for the National Association for the

Advancement of Colored People magazine *Crisis*, and suggested that blacks should concentrate on highlighting the positive contribution made by their culture on American society, as the Irish had done.

Prominent '60s student radical Tom Hayden traced his Irish roots back to County Monaghan, and for much of the mid-1960s organized a black community union in Newark. (Now a California state senator, he spent much of July 1998 with the residents of the Garvaghy Road,[13] waiting to see if the controversial Orange Order march would take place.)

An Irish priest, Fr. Eugene Boyle, was the first person to open his doors to the Black Panthers' free breakfast program in San Francisco when it began in 1969. According to the Black Panther newspaper, Boyle allowed his Sacred Heart parish facilities to be used by the Panthers for the program despite being "subjected to police intimidation and racist **epithets**[14] and slurs, ..." Boyle also allowed the Sacred Heart Church to be used for Panther memorial services and even Panther political meetings. In May 1971, he flew from California to New Haven, Connecticut to appear as a witness for Panther leader Bobby Seale, who was being tried for murder.

More famous figures like the Kennedys also identified themselves with the struggle for civil rights in the U.S., and proved very popular with black voters. Despite being physically assaulted by some of his Irish American constituents in Boston for his support of busing in 1975, Ted Kennedy has remained an unswerving advocate of black civil rights.

Robert Kennedy was particularly identified with the black struggle during his years as Senator for New York (1965–1968), and proved a remarkably popular candidate with black voters during his presidential election

---

[13] Garvaghy Road—Catholic neighborhood in Belfast, Northern Ireland.

[14] **epithets**—abusive names.

campaign in 1968. He set up a ghetto renewal scheme in the Bedford Stuyvesant ghetto of New York, continually gave financial support to militant black leader Floyd McKissick, and was one of the first major American (or foreign) politicians to go to South Africa to attack apartheid.[15]

When he landed in New York after the South Africa trip in 1966, he pointed out the similar reactions to American blacks and Irish-Americans in the U.S. "Everything that is now being said about the Negro was said about the Irish Catholics. They were useless, they were worthless, they couldn't learn anything. Why did they have to settle here? Why don't we see if we can't get boats and send them back to Ireland?" he said.

Whatever the attitudes of Irish-Americans to the black civil rights movement, activists in Northern Ireland benefited enormously from its example and direct support.

Two weeks after Bloody Sunday in January 1972—when 14 unarmed civilians were shot dead by the British Army during a civil rights march in Derry—the Southern Christian Leadership Conference, founded by Martin Luther King, dispatched senior officials to Belfast to take part in protest marches and to speak at a Northern Ireland Civil Rights Association (NICRA) meeting.

Bernard Lee, a veteran of the Atlanta sit-ins and a close associate of Martin Luther King, was part of the group which included Juanita Abernathy, wife of Rev. Ralph Abernathy, another key King confidant. Juanita Abernathy told the NICRA conference that "the struggle for Irish freedom is the same struggle as that going on in the United States."

Since then, many other prominent black American leaders have made political visits to Northern Ireland. Angela Davis was reunited with Bernadette McAliskey in 1994 when she visited Belfast to take part in a local

[15] apartheid—policy of racial segregation practiced in South Africa against nonwhites.

women's political conference. The military presence in Northern Ireland, Davis said, reminded her of apartheid South Africa.

Donald Payne, the first black American to be elected to the U.S. Congress from New Jersey, noted during his trip [to Northern Ireland] in 1995 that "What I have heard and seen here about the discrimination of Catholics is the same kind of thing that I see at home. High unemployment rates, high school drop-out rates and the sense of alienation from and resentment towards the authorities." In 1997, Payne introduced a bill in the U.S. Congress to ban the RUC[16] from using plastic bullets.

Such actions have helped intensify the identification between Nationalists in Northern Ireland with black Americans. SDLP[17] leader John Hume is among those who quote enthusiastically and liberally from Martin Luther King, and his party still sings "We Shall Overcome" at its annual conferences.

Bernadette Devlin McAliskey has become something of a legend in black political circles, and has been a frequent visitor to the U.S. since 1969 and a regular speaker at black political gatherings, highlighting the cause of both Irish Republican and black American prisoners. In 1996 she spoke at fundraisers for the black churches destroyed by racist arson attacks across the American South.

In 1997, several prominent black Americans joined the campaign for the release of Roisin McAliskey, Bernadette's daughter, from jail in Britain.

Roisin McAliskey was pregnant when arrested in November 1996, spent 15 months in various British prisons awaiting **extradition**[18] to Germany on a bombing

---

[16] RUC—Royal Ulster Constabulary, the largely Protestant police force in Northern Ireland.

[17] SDLP—Social Democratic Labor Party, predominantly Catholic, anti-violence political party in Northern Ireland.

[18] **extradition**—the legal surrendering of a person to the jurisdiction of another authority.

charge, and gave birth to a girl under harsh security conditions in May 1997.

New York's first black Mayor, David Dinkins, addressed a meeting in the city protesting Roisin's treatment, and a still radical Angela Davis spoke at a rally in San Francisco, attacking the "terrible mistreatment of Roisin McAliskey by her British captors. . . . Roisin must be freed and Northern Ireland released from the shackles of British imperialism!" Roisin McAliskey was released in March 1998.

The recent ties have also helped Irish nationalists to more easily **contextualize**[19] their political situation. During the recent clash over the proposed Orange march through Garvaghy Road, the international press often described Loyalist protesters as akin to the Ku Klux Klan, and the image of Northern Ireland Catholics as White Negroes still **resonates**[20] in much of the media.

It is a useful image for Nationalist politicians in Northern Ireland, eager for the credibility of close association with the black civil rights movement.

When Sinn Féin President Gerry Adams visited the U.S. in September 1994, he made time in his hectic schedule to visit Rosa Parks, the woman whose refusal to give up her seat on a Montgomery bus in 1955 sparked the historic bus boycott and catapulted Martin Luther King to the leadership of the civil rights movement. (The boycott was itself an Irish form of protest initiated by [county] Mayo laborers in 1880 who refused to harvest the crops of the notorious land agent Captain Charles Cunningham Boycott.)

Adams told Rosa Parks he had sung "We Shall Overcome" at the early civil rights marches in Belfast, and had been inspired by her principled and courageous stand. A few days later, Adams was hoping President

---

[19] **contextualize**—put into the circumstances or context in which an event occurs.

[20] **resonates**—resounds or reverberates.

Clinton would ignore British government protests and invite him to the White House.

Reminded of Parks' refusal to be classed as a second-class citizen 40 years before, Adams told the **intermediary**[21] between himself and the White House that he wanted an invitation, that he "would not accept a place at the back of the bus."

Adopting the vocabulary and tactics from each other's movements, and identifying with each other's struggle, is a deeply rooted tradition in both Irish and black American political culture, and has proved crucially important in Northern Ireland over the last 30 years.

---

[21] **intermediary**—mediator between two persons or groups.

QUESTIONS TO CONSIDER

1. What historical personalities and events brought the civil rights struggles in Northern Ireland and America together?

2. What convincing parallels does Dooley draw between the two groups?

3. Why do oppressed groups try to find common issues, and why do their opponents want to keep them apart?

4. What common cause might blacks and Irish Americans have in the new millennium?

Old Airs and New: From Reels to *Riverdance*

BY MICK MOLONEY

Irish-born Mick Moloney—a folk singer and musician turned scholar—holds a Ph.D. in folklore and folklife from the University of Pennsylvania. He is a teacher of ethnomusicology, folklore, and Irish studies courses at major United States' universities. He is an accomplished banjo player, and has performed on National Public Radio. He also wrote and narrated a thirteen-part series on Irish music in America for the Public Broadcasting System. Here he reviews the historic roots of Irish music and how its popularity has spread worldwide in recent decades.

In 1993, an experimental dance production called *Riverdance* was performed in Dublin on live television during the Eurovision Song Contest, before an estimated audience of 600 million Europeans. The seven-minute piece brought together newly created music with innovative Irish dance routines. The reaction was

unprecedented.[1] *Riverdance* mania swept the continent. A general European audience discovered Irish dancing, and public perception of Irish dance within Ireland was transformed, literally, overnight. No longer was it considered stiff and old-fashioned. Now it was sexy and trendy.

An elaborated version of the show was produced and the format expanded to encompass other forms of **percussive**[2] dance, including **flamenco**,[3] clogging, tap, and Russian folk ballet. The show opened in Dublin and played to capacity audiences for ten weeks. It moved to London and sold out in the West End for five months. It then arrived at Radio City Music Hall in March 1996, playing to capacity audiences of six thousand per night, and returning in late 1996 and 1997 for a nationwide tour. **Cloned**[4] versions now run simultaneously worldwide. Fortunes have already been made by composers, choreographers, artists, and producers, and international reputations have been won.

When *Riverdance* arrived in the United States it was in a sense coming home. The two principal dancers—Michael Flatley and Jean Butler—were born in America of immigrant Irish parents. Butler was born and raised in Long Island and had been studying Irish dance since she was seven; Flatley was born in Chicago and had been dancing since he was eight.

Riverdance was a public validation of a national culture on the international stage, demonstrating and celebrating the capacity of traditional Irish dance to become cosmopolitan without losing its identity. The traditional dimension came from Ireland; the innovations, from America. *Riverdance* could not have happened without both.

---

[1] **unprecedented**—like nothing before.

[2] **percussive**—striking or pounding of shoes or musical instruments to produce a rhythmic beat.

[3] **flamenco**—rhythmic Spanish folk dance.

[4] **Cloned**—duplicated, identically copied.

This tension between the old and the new, between the urge to traditionalize and the urge to innovate, has always been at the heart of the story of Irish culture in America.

At the heart of Irish culture—be it the dance, the poetry, or the language itself—is music. And for hundreds of years Irish people have expressed their deepest, most heartfelt concerns through reels, airs, and tunes. They carried this tradition with them to their new home in America—or Amerikay, as it was known in many of the thousands of songs of emigration written in the eighteenth and nineteenth centuries. Much of the music of the Appalachian Mountains was shaped by the songs and tunes brought over by immigrants from Northern Ireland in the latter decades of the eighteenth century. In the mountains of Tennessee, Kentucky, Virginia, West Virginia, and the Carolinas, Irish music came together with English, Scottish, and later African-American music. The music that emerged was known as hillbilly or old-time mountain music and is heard there to this day. The branches that grew from this early cultural influence include bluegrass and country music, both with strong Irish accents.

Many of the Irish immigrants who flocked to America in the wake of the Great Hunger in the latter decades of the nineteenth century came from the western counties, which were home to much of the traditional music of Ireland at that time. Hence a lot of traditional musicians ended up in America, and they brought their music with them.

Irish traditional music is a sophisticated, highly evolved art form. It is characteristically played on instruments such as the fiddle, uilleann pipes,[5] wooden flute,

---

[5] uilleann pipes—Irish bagpipes. Unlike Scottish Highland pipes, uilleann pipes are designed to be played indoors, sitting down, for social (not military) occasions. They produce the widest range of notes of any bagpipe.

tin whistle, accordion, concertina,[6] tenor banjo, and mandolin, often accompanied by guitar, bouzouki,[7] bodhran,[8] or bones.

The **repertoire**[9] is composed of dance music pieces such as jigs, reels, hornpipes, polkas, mazurkas,[10] flings, and waltzes and other instrumental forms such as slow airs, marches, and planxties.[11] Some pieces date from as far back as the sixteenth century, while others are more recent in origin.

In the large American cities, musicians from widely separated villages in Ireland came together, and a rich cross-fertilization of styles and repertoires ensued. These cultural traditions are now as American as they are Irish. New styles and forms developed from a new generation of Irish-American musicians in Boston, Chicago, Philadelphia, and New York. Classic 78 rpm recordings[12] were made of great Irish musicians in America between 1916 and the early 1930s.

Musicians such as uilleann piper Patsy Tuohey from Galway, the Flanagan Brothers from Waterford, Dan Sullivan's Shamrock Band from Boston, fiddlers James Morrison, Paddy Killoran, and the **incomparable**[13] Michael Coleman of Sligo recorded in the 1920s and 1930s for Victor, Columbia, Decca, and other companies. These recordings made their way back to Ireland, where they had a profound effect on the evolution of the tradition in the home country.

---

[6] concertina—small, hexagonal accordion with bellows and buttons for keys.

[7] bouzouki—musical instrument, originally used in Greece and the Balkan countries.

[8] bodhran—hand-held Irish drum.

[9] **repertoire**—stock of songs, plays, operas, or readings that a player or company is prepared to perform.

[10] mazurkas—lively Polish dances or pieces of music for such a dance.

[11] planxties—Irish songs composed for a patron.

[12] 78 rpm recordings—records that made 78 circular turns or "revolutions" per minute on a phonograph.

[13] **incomparable**—unmatchable.

By the 1960s, however, traditional music was **inexorably**[14] declining as a force in Irish-American social and cultural life, a trend hastened by changing musical tastes and diminishing immigration. The old Irish dance halls, which provided a major social outlet for the music, had long vanished from urban America.

Today, however, young American-born Irish musicians are in the forefront of the Irish music scene in this country, and when the All Ireland dance and music competitions are held each year in Ireland, Americans of Irish ancestry are sure to be among the winners. **Virtuoso**[15] young musicians are enlivening this **venerable**[16] tradition all over America, and the future for the music has never been brighter. American-born musicians such as Eileen Ivers, Seamus Egan, and Joannie Madden, leader of Cherish the Ladies, the only all-woman band in traditional Irish music, have achieved major success in the popular music market. New tunes are also being composed daily in America, adding to the great store of music that has been passed down through the centuries.

There has been a similar resurgence in purely Irish singing, owing to the commercial success of the Clancy Brothers and Tommy Makem in New York in the early 1960s. Their style was a classic hybrid, combining an Irish and Scottish song repertoire with a performance style directly derived from the American folk song revival. Their success was instant and meteoric, catapulting them to international stardom and creating overnight a commercial market for a new **genre**[17] of Irish song culture in America and also back in Ireland. Audiences found their new rhythmic approach to the

---

[14] **inexorably**—relentlessly, not able to be stopped.

[15] **Virtuoso**—masterful; extraordinarily talented.

[16] **venerable**—worthy of reverence or respect by virtue of dignity, character, or age.

[17] **genre**—category of art distinguished by a definite style, form, or content.

performing of Irish songs and their novel use of harmonies along with guitar and five-string banjo accompaniment refreshing and captivating. Their legacy can be found in the profusion of Irish groups now performing in Irish bars across America—a **milieu**[18] in which many Americans hear Irish singing for the first time.

Today there are more places in America where Irish music and dance are performed than in Ireland. One can enjoy them at festivals, events sponsored by cultural and arts organizations, colleges, museums, and historical societies. National Public Radio and PBS [the Public Broadcasting System] bring Irish traditional music weekly to millions of Americans, many of them classical music lovers—a situation that would have seemed impossible twenty years ago. The captains of the ethnopop industry are now eagerly exploiting the "Celtic" **market niche**,[19] and a steady stream of Irish recordings have reached the top **echelons**[20] of the world music charts all through the 1990s. Irish rock groups fill the airwaves, and Ireland's most famous rock group, U2, continues to fill the biggest stadiums in the land every time they tour the States. Grammys are handed out annually to Irish musicians and composers. Irish films such as *The Commitments* have achieved cult status among the young. All over America Irish pubs thrive, with live Irish music providing a backdrop to the animated gossip of the crowds who flock to them in record numbers. The country becomes greener with every passing Saint Patrick's Day. In fact, just about everything Irish is in America as the millennium approaches.

---

[18] **milieu**—environment or surroundings.

[19] **market niche**—special area of demand for a product or service.

[20] **echelons**—ranks.

Which brings us back to the healthy tension between the old and the new. Doing things in a traditional way involves taking responsibility for the future and also being respectful of the past. This is a truly humble act but also a supremely **assertive**[21] one.

---

[21] **assertive**—inclined to be bold and direct; positive.

QUESTIONS TO CONSIDER

1. How do music and dance help with a group's cultural assimilation?

2. How has the United States helped to preserve traditional Irish song and dance?

3. Moloney says that many Irish Famine immigrants were from the western counties of Ireland and that this was home to much of the traditional music. This was also the area where Gaelic (Irish) was spoken more widely than English. How are language and music linked in an oral tradition?

Diversity Blarney

BY PETE HAMILL

In 1999 housing officials in Boston—a city with a large Irish-American population and a long history of racial unrest—created a public debate by declaring an ancient Irish symbol, the shamrock, to be insensitive and controversial. Pete Hamill, an Irish-American novelist and former newspaper editor, looks at this issue and the whole concept of ethnic diversity in America in this article he wrote for The Wall Street Journal.

There is another one of those peculiarly American uproars now under way in Boston, and it would be immensely entertaining if it weren't so wasteful and stupid. It seems that the Boston Housing Authority has been operating a "diversity program," another bureaucratic endeavor with the usual honorable intention, to improve human behavior. In this case, the goal is to make residents of public housing projects more sensitive to the feelings of their neighbors. In particular, they want the project dwellers to understand the effect that certain publicly flaunted symbols can have on others. Among those "controversial decorations" are the Confederate and Puerto Rican flags, the **swastika**[1] and the shamrock.

The shamrock?

Yes: the shamrock.

The Boston Housing Authority being in Boston, and Boston being a city with large numbers of citizens who trace their ancestry to Ireland, this inclusion in the curriculum of the diversity program led to the uproar. Some Irish-Americans were furious at being linked with the swastika. Others were insulted at being joined with the adolescent **yahoos**[2] who lurch around football parking lots waving the flag of the Confederacy. Most were probably baffled by the inclusion of the flag of Puerto Rico. But the shamrock?

For many Irish-Americans (I'm one of them), the shamrock is part of the green-beer-kiss-me-I'm-Irish nonsense that engulfs us all on St. Patrick's Day and causes some of us to stay home, lock the door, and watch a Fellini movie. When we see a plastic shamrock, our hearts don't swell with pride or defiance; we don't inflate with a rush of self-importance; we don't cheer or weep. We are indifferent. Usually, the pasting of a shamrock upon the signboard of some bogus Irish pub is a symbol of only one thing: a complete and utter failure of imagination. To be sure, we are not indifferent to all of this fraudulent, pre-fabricated Irishness. Sometimes we even act. Whenever I hear some **paunchy**[3] tenor rise to bellow "Danny Boy," I usually knock over chairs on my way to the door. I am not alone.

To be fair to the good bureaucrats of the Boston Housing Authority, they might have included the shamrock for other reasons: to defuse the fear it might

---

[1] **swastika**—emblem of Nazi Germany, later adopted by white extremist groups elsewhere.

[2] **yahoos**—crude, brutish people, named after a race of humanlike brutes in *Gulliver's Travels* by Jonathan Swift.

[3] **paunchy**—pot-bellied.

unwittingly inspire among Americans whose ancestors did not come from Mullingar or Mayo. But that means that in a true discussion of the shamrock they would have to explain that it is a **hoary**,[4] empty device that now symbolizes almost nothing. It is not a Celtic symbol (which in Boston would grant it a certain power, now temporarily in recession). A vague mixture of legend and folklore traces it to fifth century Ireland and the arrival of St. Patrick, who used it to explain the concept of the Holy Trinity. But Patrick was French, not Irish, so the shamrock could as easily be a symbol of French Christianity as it is of Irishness.

No matter what its origins (and there were no reporters present making notes), today the shamrock has no real meaning beyond the sentimental. It has no political importance. It doesn't represent Sinn Féin or the Irish Republican Army. It doesn't adorn the Irish flag. The shamrock today only reflects the Irish-American past.

Much of that past was bitter, for the Irish came here from a country whose entire modern history was the story of an oppressed majority. In the U.S., they were met with anti-Irish bigotry that was real, wounding, and sometimes dangerous. As late as the first decades of this century, the "wearing of the green" was often an act of defiance. It said to the Anglo-Saxon majority, "I'm Irish, I'm proud of it, and I'm here to stay—so what are you going to do about it?"

But that era is long gone, brought to an abrupt end by the election of Jack Kennedy in 1960. Someone once said, without complete approval, that Kennedy was more Harvard than Southie,[5] and that was absolutely true. His presence, his intelligence, his wit, his sense of irony announced a new way of being Irish-American, and he got rid of the Stage Irishman forever. That

---

[4] **hoary**—ancient.

[5] Southie—nickname for someone from South Boston, a predominantly Irish-American working class area.

sure-and-begorrah stereotype, full of blarney and whiskey and adorned with shamrocks, had been invented (alas, by Irishmen themselves), as a means of protection against the people of power. If you could reassure the powerful that you were ineffectual, lazy, **impotent**[6] or drunk, they would laugh at you, and while laughing, do you no harm. Kennedy got rid of that stereotype the way Jackie Robinson in 1947 got rid of Stepin Fetchit[7] and his, shuffling **servility**.[8]

All of that is worth discussing in the projects operated by the Boston Housing Authority, and in other forums of public discourse. But it will be quite difficult in the present climate. All such discussion has been poisoned by the wormy self-pity that is at the core of identity politics. The genius of the American experience has been its great leveling power. Human beings from a great variety of cultures arrived here, collided, went to schools or wars together, married each other, and built an amazing country. Most of them were too busy to feel sorry for themselves. Much of that healthy attitude has eroded. Today, we too often find Americans whose essential slogan is, "I'm offended, therefore I am."

That oh-woe-is-me attitude is paralyzing. If you believe the deck is stacked from birth, then why bother struggling? If you think that you will never have a real chance at a full life because you are a woman, a homosexual, short, bald, or fat, or if your ancestors came from Africa or spoke Spanish, you will never have that real chance because you will not take it. If you reduce yourself to some sociological category instead of being fully human, you will also be building your own little psychic jail. No human being is simply Irish, gay, African, or bald; if they were, nobody would write novels.

---

[6] **impotent**—powerless.

[7] Stepin Fetchit—stage name of an African-American film actor who in the 1920s and 1930s played stereotypical roles that demeaned blacks.

[8] **servility**—submissiveness.

But if you are such a sensitive soul that you are frozen into fear, or moved to anger, by the existence of evil, **banal**,[9] or meaningless symbols, then this rough American democracy has nothing to offer to you or your children. Here we must bump up against much idiocy and laugh it into the **ashpit**.[10] A handful of Irish-Americans might feel nostalgia for the days when they were true victims, but in doing so they become comic figures, devoid of **irony**.[11]

Those Irish-Americans who refused the slippery embrace of self-pity now run huge corporations and media conglomerates; they have distinguished themselves in journalism, literature, the theater and the movies; in a country where the beginning was often nasty and brutalizing, they have won all the late rounds. For most of them that I've met, the enemies are the traditional ones: stupidity, narrowness, cruelty. With all their power and material success, they have not forgotten where they came from. They have remained true to the Irish traditions of generosity to the stranger, the afflicted, and the hungry without for a moment feeling they must brandish a shamrock as [a] badge of identity.

If the true story of the Irish in America could be told in the Boston projects—and in the rest of this country—we'd all be better off. After all, it is an American story, not an Irish story. Of course, if we pretend to be educated, we should know the stories of all the other groups that share this country but not in the narrow ways such tales are now too often being narrated, as mere catalogs of injustices.

The true story of every group—told widely and not narrowly—is both enriching and consoling. We always

---

[9] **banal**—worn-out convention or type; predictable and commonplace.

[10] **ashpit**—garbage heap.

[11] **irony**—use of words to convey the opposite of their literal meaning.

learn that beyond superficial differences (flags, language, music, food) we are much more like each other than we are different. The newspapers of the world are filled with the same tales of human folly. The myths, sagas, songs and literature of the world teach us that every society on earth contains its own collection of fools, boors, liars, cheats and brutes, along with a great majority of fundamentally decent men and women, and a tiny minority of people who are brilliant. Any education worth having, from Harvard to Southie, is about that kind of diversity. It could even explore the lost meanings of dead symbols.

QUESTIONS TO CONSIDER

1. What is the Irish-American stereotype that Hamill associates with the shamrock?

2. Why is Hamill against the politics of identity?

3. What type of diversity does Hamill favor?

Will It Ever Be 'Wonderful Here'?

BY FATHER MICHAEL DOYLE

Father Doyle, a Roman Catholic priest, was born in 1934 on a farm in County Longford, Ireland. He was educated at St. Peter's Seminary in Wexford and ordained a priest in 1959. He was recruited from the seminary for the Diocese of Camden, New Jersey, in 1959 and became a high school teacher and assistant pastor in various parishes in the diocese. In 1971, he participated in a protest against the Vietnam War at the Federal Building in Camden. He was arrested along with twenty-seven others, who were called the "Camden 28." He was acquitted two years later in a trial where he acted as his own defense lawyer. In 1974, he was appointed pastor of Sacred Heart Parish in Camden and later founded a free medical clinic for the poor and a program that renovates abandoned houses and sells them without profit or interest to low-income families. Doyle has written both prose and poetry about his Irish roots and about Camden, including this letter to parishioners.

February 1999

Hi:

In January, 1983 Harry Reasoner and CBS' "60 Minutes" came to Sacred Heart and produced a segment which aired on March 20 and was entitled "Michael Doyle's Camden." As you might expect it criticized the powerful forces that have placed all Camden County's 'unwantables' in terms of hindrance to real estate enhancement and profit among the poor people of Camden. For example, forty-six sewer plants were shut down in Camden County[1] and all the sewage and its horrific odors are now treated in Camden City, plus all the **incineration**[2] of garbage, plus prisons, et cetera, et cetera. It was not a pleasant picture that beamed out to the nation in 1983 but it was a true one.

Most of the blame for conditions inside the city was placed on raw power and indifference outside it. After the airing, many local **movers and shakers**[3] reacted angrily. Today most of the very vocal have long since left the city and some who represented the corporate sector have not only left but their industries have left, too. The piece itself was criticized as being journalistically **subjective**.[4] Maybe it was. It did, however, win an Emmy for CBS.

Mixed among the many pictures of Camden that flashed across the screen from the happy bottle-breaking ceremonies of [First Lady] Mamie Eisenhower 'christening' the *Savannah* at the nearby shipyard in July of 1959 before fifteen thousand people (the *Savannah* was the first nuclear-powered cargo and passenger ship in the world) to the **desolate**[5] heart-breaking scenes of urban

---

[1] Camden County—the suburban, wealthier areas surrounding the city of Camden.

[2] **incineration**—burning.

[3] **movers and shakers**—powerful individuals.

[4] **subjective**—one-sided, unbalanced.

[5] **desolate**—devastating.

desolation that scarred the **maligned**[6] face of Camden in 1983 were these words: "For Ash Wednesday, Harry Reasoner," I said, "for Ash Wednesday I would like to get this dirt that they say is Camden and just put that on the foreheads of this society and say: THINK! Why is this place the way it is?"

The years have gone by. Many faces of the elderly that "60 Minutes" filmed at Mass in Sacred Heart are gone today and so are the factories of Campbell Soup and R.C.A. which Harry Reasoner described then as "going strong."

Now it's Ash Wednesday 1999, the last one before the bells begin to ring for the heart-pounding realization of the awesome moment, 2000 A.D. On February 17, with only three hundred and eighteen days to go before the cosmic silence shatters, we gathered at Sacred Heart and put ashes on our foreheads in Camden. Not for us the clean easy ashes of last year's burned palm! NO! We went out (we didn't have to go far) and brought back some of the ashes of a burned-out building. Plenty of them nearby. More than three thousand abandoned homes pock mark the face of this once-thriving city. Many of them incinerated shells. Looking over a list of some of the fires that blackened these skies across many years is like calling ghosts from the embers of the way we were. Back in 1856 the ferryboat *New Jersey* burned while crossing the Delaware here and fifty people lost their lives. The Miller-Rittenhouse licorice factory at the foot of Jefferson Street burned in 1902. The shipping department of Victor Talking Machine in 1904. Mickle Street Armory in 1906 (three firemen died). The Y.M.C.A. also in 1932. The huge Hollingshead Factory in 1940 (ten people died). The Linden Baptist church in 1953. Camden Catholic High School in 1960. In the riots of 1971 Broadway went up in flames. And over the past

---

[6] **maligned**—slandered; defamed.

thirty years numerous fires have consumed homes and blocks and businesses. Scores of people have been killed. Many of them children. The saddest duty of my whole life was entering Camden morgue in 1971 to identify Joe McCann and his five little children. All killed by fire in their home. Fire is a frequent cruel killer in urban poverty.

So I say again, the light dust of the palm is hardly enough for an Ash Wednesday in Camden. It does call us to repent our broken promises but the ashes of Camden in a deep and organic way portray the broken promise of the nation of which we are all a part. As I often say, Camden is the best visual aid in America for what has gone wrong and is still going wrong. The casualty of the progress. The sorrow in the success. The starvation in the surplus.

Many of those who came to Sacred Heart for ashes care about Camden. It's not easy to care enough. The "60 Minutes" piece proclaimed that if "Jesus cried over Jerusalem, he would scream over Camden." But wearing the ashes of its ruins in faith is a cry for its transformation, for our transformation, for resurrection of life from death. A little African American girl came into Sacred Heart Church today for the first time walking in front of her mother. She paused, looked around at the newly renovated church, and lifted up her little six-year-old arms. Then in a loud voice and in sheer delight, said "Oh, it's wonderful here."

Each year during the month of November we remember the dead in a special way at Mass in Sacred Heart and on the last Sunday of that month of memories, we call out the names of those who were murdered. We pray and light a candle for each one of those who fell in the annual slaughter of our city. The name, the age, the weapon. . . thirty-nine from November '97 to November '98 in this town of eighty-five thousand people. Blood on whose hands! I'm not sure. But ashes on our heads is good. It is a start. A realization. A cry to God to change our hearts. To change the national direction. I wish I could put some of these Camden ashes on the forehead of our present President of the United States. On July 17, 1992, about fifteen hours after he was nominated in New York City, William Jefferson Clinton made his first stop on his journey to the White House in Camden, NJ. Chances are, he's never thought of it since. (Did I read somewhere that he likes Walt Whitman's *Leaves of Grass*?[7]) Yet, in the past seven years perhaps two hundred and fifty citizens have been murdered in this little urban concentration of poverty. Strange words these are in times of economic success and national surplus. Political questions and disagreements are now arising as to what to do with it. The military will certainly get more. It has too much. Drug enforcement will get more. It will get nowhere. Social Security will be strengthened and it should.

But the Camdens of this nation! The urban and rural wastelands of poverty where so many citizens are killed. What of them! Thank God our young people are not dying right now on frontiers or front lines far away. But they are dying on the back alleys of urban America.

I am writing this in church with a rough, blackened thumb from daubing ashes on foreheads, black and white and brown, calling to you to focus your faith on the ashes of Camden as we move on towards this great millennium of time. Pray that America will come to the front lines of our cities to protect our children not with guns but with hammers and saws and jobs and tools of transformation.

O God, grant that someday the ashes will be washed from the face of our city, that it will be rebuilt and renewed, that little Camden children will look at it as God always willed they would, raise their arms in sheer delight and say, "It's wonderful here."

Sincerely,
Michael Doyle

---

[7] Walt Whitman was a nineteenth-century American poet, born in Camden.

QUESTIONS TO CONSIDER

1. What are the likely effects of concentrating sewage treatment plants, garbage incinerators, and prisons in a poverty-stricken city?

2. What is the symbolism of the ashes Father Doyle uses on Ash Wednesday?

3. How can we prevent murders with hammers, saws, and jobs?

Scraps and Leftovers: A Meditation

BY FRANK McCOURT

Frank McCourt is an author whose memoir of childhood, Angela's Ashes, *won many important literary awards, including the Pulitzer Prize for biography. McCourt was born to newly arrived Irish immigrants in Depression-era Brooklyn. After the death of his baby sister, the family decided to return to Ireland, where he was raised amid the poverty of Limerick. As a young man, he returned to New York, served in the U.S. Army, and became a high school teacher in New York City. In* Angela's Ashes *he wrote: "When I look back on my childhood I wonder how I managed to survive at all. It was, of course, a miserable childhood; the happy childhood is hardly worth your while. Worse than the ordinary miserable childhood is the miserable Irish childhood, and worse yet is the miserable Irish Catholic childhood."*

If you grew up in Ireland you were told about the famine. It was **dinned**[1] into you. In the history books there were pictures of huddled families dying of hunger in their **hovels**,[2] the same families being evicted—by English landlords—and with no place to go but a ditch.

In the 1930s and 1940s old people in Limerick City still whispered of the horrors of that famine less than 100 years before. They said it was the fault of the English. They said it was a fact that tons of corn were shipped out of the country to feed Her Majesty's armies beyond. There was enough food to go around to feed Ireland ten times over.

The old people said they would never forgive that of the English and they hoped we wouldn't either.

Now the pope himself is talking along the same lines. He's saying there's enough food for everyone and that's supposed to squelch the arguments of the pro-choice people, who might claim there's an awful scarcity of vital stuffs in this world, of both love and food.

But the pope's right. Isn't the pope always right? There is enough to go around. Surely everyone knows that and isn't it **banal**[3] even to say it? Hannah Arendt[4] spoke of the banality of evil: had she devised a catalogue of banality she might have included hunger.

When you talk of hunger you can't avoid talking of its opposite—excess. All over America there are restaurant signs inviting you inside to eat all you can for less than ten dollars and there are cars, large cars, driving up to **disgorge**[5] people so **obese**[6] they can hardly get out the door or in the door.

---

[1] **dinned**—uttered with persistent repetition.

[2] **hovels**—wretched huts.

[3] **banal**—worn-out from repetition, trite, commonplace, and drearily predictable.

[4] Hannah Arendt—philosopher who wrote about Nazi Germany and its persecution of Jews.

[5] **disgorge**—to discharge or pour forth contents.

[6] **obese**—fat.

As an English teacher in various New York City high schools I was often assigned to "cafeteria duty." I was to patrol the students' lunchroom, make sure they behaved themselves, break up fights, tell them to take their trays back and to clean up around their tables.

I watched them eat and drink. I listened to them complain about the food as they dumped their untouched lunches into the garbage. I saw them sneak out of school to various fast-food joints in the neighborhood.

It was a film rerun from my army days: the moaning and [complaining] over food in Camp Kilmer and Fort Dix, New Jersey, and in a soldier's mess hall in Bavaria.

From GI days to teacher days I stood in awe of the delicate and discriminating **palates**[7] of American youth. I shook my head when kids in American films had to be coaxed to eat their hamburgers. I wished I could have so loftily rejected real food. In the army, I wished I could have whimpered for Mom's delicious dishes. Instead I just whimpered.

My mother, in our Limerick City slum, had neither food nor dishes. We lived mostly on bread and tea, a solid and a liquid, a balanced diet, and what more do you want?

As soldier or teacher I wanted to yell, "Shut up. Eat your [expletive] food. There are millions starving everywhere this very minute." I wanted to ransack the garbage, retrieve discarded food, wrap it, ship it to Africa, India, Mexico.

Wasn't it Michael Harrington[8] who told us, through the powerful voice of John F. Kennedy, that millions of American children go to bed hungry?

In the racial unconscious of the Irish there must be some demon tormenting us over food. Mention Irish

[7] **palates**—senses of taste.
[8] Michael Harrington—Irish-American writer and expert on U.S. poverty whose works were first brought to wide public attention in the speeches of President John F. Kennedy.

cuisine and most Americans will laugh and sputter, "Yeah, corned beef an' cabbage," and we'll have to admit that up until recently we've had an uneasy relationship with food. Our forebears, landing on the eastern seaboard of the United States, hesitated to move inland, where they could have farmed to their hearts' content. Oh, no, they weren't going to be caught again. Look at what the land had done to them in Ireland. They'd stay in the big cities, never again be victims of the treacherous **spud**.[9] Irishmen worked in construction: the buildings, the canals, the railroads. They were ignorant of food. The Irishman drank—and died early. Irishwomen—Brigids, Marys, Mollys—worked in the great houses of the rich in New York and Boston. They learned to clean and stitch and sew, to pour wine and to cook the best of foods. They lived long lives and left money for their children to go to school and learn how to sell insurance. Historians tell us those servant girls sent money to the Old Country far in excess of what women from other countries sent to *their* countries. Was there enough to go around, then?

In Irish-American literature there isn't much about poverty, never mind hunger. We don't have the Dickens who wrote in his *American Notes* of the horrors of the infamous Five Points, a notorious Irish/African slum near what is now Chinatown in New York (by Irish-slash-African I mean the population of **indigent**[10] Irish and runaway slaves living in riotous **miscegenation**[11]). A **connoisseur**[12] of "poverty" writing could go to James Plunkett's *Strumpet City* or George Orwell's *The Road to Wigan Pier*. Alone among Irish-American writers, William Kennedy, in *Ironweed*, evokes the stink and

---

[9] **spud**—slang term for potato.

[10] **indigent**—impoverished; poor.

[11] **miscegenation**—interbreeding or intermarriage between persons of different races.

[12] **connoisseur**—expert on matters of taste or art.

desperation of poverty. Or you could go back to Upton Sinclair's *The Jungle.*

The famine is over, we're well fed now; we're sniffing and sending back the wine. Here we are on the threshold of a new century looking forward and, since we're Irish, looking back.

"We don't forget, Joxer.[13] We don't forget."

We may have been baptized in the Catholic way with a splash on the forehead but we've received total immersion in Irish history. We learned the songs and the poetry and we are expected to suffer **retroactively**.[14] We were told then, and we know it now, the famine was the worst thing ever to happen to the Irish race.

I recently wrote a book in which hunger of the physical type is a major theme but I wanted to show the psychological effects of hunger, how it breaks you, how it hinders any kind of emotional development. You can think of nothing but your belly. You're an animal.

When I was nine my mother got a job in Limerick cleaning a judge's house. That Sunday we had boiled bacon, cabbage, boiled potatoes, and, for dessert, jelly and custard. For the next day she saved three boiled potatoes and some jelly and custard and placed them on a windowsill which served as the **larder**.[15]

Next day I was the first one home. I thought I'd taste the jelly and maybe the custard. I did. I thought I'd have half a potato.

You can imagine the rest. I didn't stop till everything was gone.

I ran away and slept in a hayloft outside Limerick, I could hardly sleep with the worry and the guilt and knew I had to go home. My mother was sitting by the

---

[13] "We don't forget, Joxer."— an allusion to Sean O'Casey's play *Juno and the Paycock* in which two characters are reflecting on Ireland's grim history.

[14] **retroactively**—after the fact; looking back in time.

[15] **larder**—room or cupboard where meat and other foods are kept.

fire as usual. She didn't stir but said, "Frankie, you must have been very hungry to eat everything like that."

"I was," I said.

"You know your brothers were hungry, too," said my mother.

"I suppose they were."

"Well, you're going on ten and growing and I don't think you'd ever do the likes of that again, would you?"

"I wouldn't," said I.

But I would and did in other places and I'm not a bit sorry because there's enough to go around. And there always *was* enough to go around.

QUESTIONS TO CONSIDER

1. How does McCourt propose to discuss world hunger when it has become commonplace to say there is enough food to go around?

2. Why was McCourt "in awe of the delicate and discriminating palates of American youth"?

3. McCourt says, "The famine is over, we're well fed now; we're sniffing and sending back the wine." What does this sentence imply about the Irish and the lessons of the Famine?

Texts

158 "The High Divers" by Jack Conroy (1898–1990). Courtesy of Douglas Wixson and the Jack Conroy Memorial Collection, Moberly Area Community College, Moberly, Missouri 65270.

167 "Immigrant Daughter's Song" by Mary Ann Larkin. Copyright Mary Ann Larkin. Reprinted by permission.

170 "Mark O'Brien, 49, Journalist And Poet in Iron Lung, is Dead", by William H. Honan *The New York Times,* Sunday, July 11,1999. Copyright © 1999 by the New York Times Co. Reprinted by permission.

172 Poem from *Breathing* by Mark O'Brien. Copyright © 1998 Lemonade Factory, Berkeley, CA. Used by permission.

184 From "Black and Green: The historic connection between black American civil rights activists and Irish nationalists" by Brian Dooley from *Irish America Magazine,* Sept./Oct. 1998. Brian Dooley is author of *Black and Green: The Fight for Civil Rights in Northern Ireland and Black America,* Pluto Press, 1998. Reprinted by permission of the author.

197 "Old Airs and New: From Reels to *Riverdance*" by Mick Moloney. Copyright © 1997 by Mick Moloney. Reprinted by permission of Mick Moloney, Ph.D.

204 Reprinted with permission of Dow Jones from "Diversity Blarney" by Pete Hamill in *The Wall Street Journal,* August 12, 1999; permission conveyed through Copyright Clearance Center, Inc.

210 "Will It Ever Be 'Wonderful Here'?" from *Monthly Letters from the Heart* by Michael Doyle, Pastor of Sacred Heart Church, Camden, NJ 08104. Reprinted by permission of the author.

216 From *The Irish in America,* edited by Michael Coffey. Copyright © 1997 by Disney Enterprises, Inc. "Scraps and Leftovers: A Meditation," Copyright © 1997 by Frank McCourt. Reprinted by permission of Hyperion Books.

Images

Photo Research Diane Hamilton

10 © Wolfhound Press Ltd., Dublin

49 *top,* **50** *top,* **51** *bottom,* **52, 68–69, 106, 109–112, 145, 146, 149, 174, 175** *top,* **180–181** Courtesy Library of Congress.

49 *bottom* © University College Dublin—Dept. of Irish Folklore.

107 © Chicago Historical Society.

108 *top,* © Geo. Topp/Courtesy of Ben/Trade Card Place (The).

108 *bottom,* 148 © Brown Brothers.

147, 176–177 © AP/Wide World Photos.

150 © Boys Town Hall of History Collection/Father Flanagan's Boys' Home

175 *bottom,* **178** © Photofest.

179 *top* © Archive Photo.

179 *bottom* © Hulton-Deutsch Collection/Corbis.

182 © Michael Brennan/Corbis.

Every effort has been made to secure complete rights and permissions for each selection presented herein. Updated acknowledgements, if needed, will appear in subsequent printings.

Index